FOREWORD

DR. KAREN MCLEAN, PHD, LMSW

THERAPISTS UNMASKED

True Stories of Resilience, Transformation, and Breaking Barriers Beyond a Diagnosis

THE VISIONARY AUTHOR

TANGIE R. MCDOUGALD, LPC

Published by McDougald Enterprises, LLC.

Therapists Unmasked: True Stories of Resilience, Transformation, and Breaking Barriers Beyond a Diagnosis is authored by licensed mental health professionals who share personal stories and insights into their healing journeys. This book is curated to reduce disparities surrounding mental health by providing vulnerable, relatable narratives from professional helpers, aiming to foster connection, reduce stigma, and promote mental health awareness.

While some chapters include strategies that contributors have found helpful in their own lives, this book is not intended to serve as clinical advice or therapeutic guidance. The content is for informational and inspirational purposes only and reflects the individual experiences of the contributors. It is not a substitute for professional mental health treatment, diagnosis, or consultation. Readers are encouraged to seek personalized care from a qualified therapist or healthcare provider for their specific needs.

DISCLOSURE

Manuscript Editing
Renee Y. Reliford
reneeyvette531@gmail.com

Book Cover Design
Ellese & Co Creative
www.elleseandco.com

ISBN for Paperback: 979-8-9921050-0-1
ISBN for E-book: 979-8-9921050-1-8
Library of Congress Control Number: 2024926279

DEDICATION

Mental health is more than a diagnosis; it's a journey—one marked by courage, vulnerability, and profound transformation.

Therapists Unmasked brings together the voices of trailblazing mental health professionals who have dared to confront their own challenges while guiding others through theirs. In a world where therapists are often seen as untouchable pillars of stability, the authors of this anthology bravely unmask themselves, revealing the personal struggles with anxiety, grief, trauma, and identity that they, too, face. They remind us that behind every professional mask lies a human heart, burdened by the very issues they help their clients navigate.

This book is dedicated to those who seek to strengthen their well-being and push through life's adversities. May it inspire resilience, healing, and hope on your journey.

To my family—my mother, my spouse, my children, and my grandchildren and those who will follow in our lineage—you are my foundation, my inspiration, and my greatest blessing.

Mom, you have been the head of the table, the diamond in the rough, carrying the torch passed down by our ancestors who stood against oppression, fought for what was right, and advocated for change. To my spouse, thank you for standing by my side through every challenge and triumph. To my children and grandchildren, may this work remind you of the strength that runs through our family and inspire you to carry this legacy forward.

To the therapists who are brave enough to unmask in order to heal—may you find strength in your vulnerability and be empowered to seek the mental health services you need when needed.

A special dedication to my sister, Laverne Michelle—honoring your love, legacy, and your children. Your strength continues to inspire me, and your memory lives on through this work and the lives you've touched.

#TherapistsUnmasked

Table of Contents

FOREWORD
DR. KAREN MCLEAN, PHD, LMSW

How many of us have thought, "I'm the expert—I should have it all together. What would it look like if I sought help? Can you imagine if my clients knew my struggle?" These thoughts are all too common for many mental health professionals. As healers, we often wear the mask of strength, even when we're struggling ourselves. The truth is, about a third of Americans—more than 43 million people—receive counseling for mental health issues each year. While therapists are the pillars of support for many, we sometimes neglect our own mental health needs.

Mental health professionals are tasked with empowering clients to navigate their challenges, create change, and build resilience. Yet, many of us face similar struggles behind the scenes. But we don't talk about it. We don't share it. And, in many cases, we don't seek the help we need. The reasons for this are layered and complex: stigma, cultural traditions of keeping things "in the family," societal rejection, shame, and, perhaps most dangerous of all—denial.

When we as professionals don't acknowledge our own mental health struggles, the consequences can be severe. Untreated mental health issues lead to burnout, emotional exhaustion, physical health problems, and even self-harm or suicide. What's more, our unaddressed struggles can also affect our clients. If we're not willing to confront and heal our own wounds, how can we truly show up for those we serve? It's crucial that we give ourselves grace—the same grace we so often encourage our clients to practice. This grace allows us to prioritize self-care, seek treatment when needed, and, most importantly, recognize that we are human.

Sharing one's vulnerability as a mental health professional is no easy task. It requires courage to look inward and to be honest about the struggles we face. The stories in this anthology shine a light on six remarkable individuals who not only help others heal but have bravely confronted their own mental health challenges. These stories are powerful testaments to the strength it takes to balance the emotional labor of supporting others while maintaining their own well-being.

As professionals, we often show up for our clients while hiding our personal pain. For the public, we wear our professional "hats," keeping our struggles hidden beneath the surface. But in this book, these professionals are choosing to take off those hats, revealing the real, raw stories underneath. This anthology is not only a source of healing for those who provide care but also a beacon for the entire community.

These personal stories delve deep into the souls of the writers, offering insight into the real-life challenges of mental health work. Along the way, they provide wisdom, inspiration, and practical lessons for self-reflection and growth. More importantly, this book aims to do more than just share experiences—it seeks to normalize conversations about mental health in our communities. It challenges the stigma, breaks the silence, and shows that even those who offer help need help too.

As you read these narratives, may you be inspired to reflect, to heal, and to advocate for a world where mental health is embraced, not hidden. This anthology serves as a platform for change—a movement toward mental health awareness and support, not just for providers, but for all.

Dr. Karen McLean, PhD, LMSW
Educator
kb73021@gmail.com
Instagram: @dockayb

Tangie R. McDougald, LPC

The Weight of Grief, the Strength of Love

Tangie R. McDougald, LPC

The Weight of Grief, the Strength of Love

"Blessed are those who mourn, for they will be comforted." Matthew 5:4 (NIV)

Under normal circumstances a "women's intuition" is something that is celebrated as a gift. It's a notion that women are more emotionally in tune, empathetic, or sensitive to the subtleties of human behavior. It's more than a gut feeling. It's a blend of experience, subconscious processing, and emotional intelligence.

The Last Call: When Grief Strikes

When my cell phone rang, I immediately became numb. My heart raced fast and it felt like I had taken my last breath. Nervous, scared and confused, I just knew the call I was getting was bad news. I was at work and in the middle of training a new employee. I let the phone ring as I felt an unsettled knot in my stomach. This took place two more times before I decided to answer. It was my oldest sister on the line. She said I needed to get to Saint Francis Hospital. The ambulance was about to transport Michelle there. She was found unconscious. I don't recall taking a breath. I muttered, "okay," and hung up the phone.

It was as if I was working on autopilot. I felt my heart racing but everything around me felt like a movie. I kept training and ignored the fact that I had to leave and head to the hospital. It was as if I was trying to delay the reality. The irrational part of me thought, "If I take my time and just finish up my day at work, my sister would be okay." Meanwhile, I knew that was not the case. My heart skipped another beat as my cell phone rang again. While trying to keep my cool, I internally cried, "No, please. Phone stop ringing; no! I looked at the phone ringing and wanted it to stop. I thought, if I ignored it, the call would go away. I just needed life to stop. I needed life to just give me a minute. I needed this urgent call to go away. See, I'm the big little sister and I always make things right. This time was different. When the phone rang and I saw it was my niece calling, I knew it was bad news. Feeling defeated, I answered. I can't remember the words that were said, but I was summoned to get to the hospital immediately.

I'm not sure how I got to the hospital. I mean, I know I drove but everything seemed so unclear. I recall pulling up in the hospital parking lot. Some of my family members were outside but when I saw my brother's car, reality hit me and I was back in the moment. My stomach felt like it was in my back and my heart was beating rapidly. Unable to catch my breath, a powerful surge of energy screamed from the pit of my stomach. It was so raw and untamed. I wished I could stop it but it had to be released. I felt like I was exploding from the inside out. I felt so heavy and didn't remember parking or getting out of my car. As I walked toward the emergency room, I could hear family members talking to me as I passed by. It sounded like they were speaking another language because I couldn't make out what was being said. They were just figures that faded in and out. I couldn't make out what was happening because everything seemed to be spinning.

I walked through the emergency room doors and was immediately rushed to her bedside where she lay motionless. My entire life flashed before me. Flashes of us taking long bubble baths together and playing "Miss Mary Mack" in the tub. Practicing the words of the Lord's Prayer. We would take turns reciting, "Our father which art in heaven, hallowed be thy name." There flashed another vision of us singing her favorite church song. She sang it loud as she stepped side to side in her white dress with a black string tie in the front. Her hair in a Jheri Curl, smiling and belting proudly, she sang, "Sign me up on a Christian Jubilee." In the background, I replied, "Write my name on the roll." Together we sang, " For I've been changed since the Lord has lifted me; I want to be ready when Jesus comes." We banged our tambourines loudly, as the entire church rejoiced to the words of the song. The song faded and the rejoicing stopped. Doctors were coming in and out of the room. People were talking to me, but I couldn't recall what they were saying. I scanned her body as she laid there. I remember my niece calling me over to her asking me to take a call. It was the coroner's office asking about the transporting of her body and conducting an autopsy. This was all too much. My head was spinning so I don't remember what I said to the coroner's office. Everything was at a standstill once I looked to the right. My eyes finally connected to hers. Laying there she looked flawless and at peace. I thought, "How can you be at peace and I'm in shambles?" It was the calmness of her children that let me know she was okay. I began to understand that she was at peace. Everything about her was perfect.

Michelle was a fashionista and one thing you were never going to do was catch her slipping. This day was no different. Her skin was smooth as butter. Her hair was freshly corn rolled in my favorite color of blue. She had her eyelashes done, nails done, jewelry on, and a fresh pair of kicks. If you knew my sister, you would understand. She was the epitome of stay ready so you don't have to get ready. Michelle took great pride in her appearance even as she transitioned.

The Crushing Reality of Loss

As I reflect on all that has taken place, one of the hardest things for me to admit is that she has served her purpose here on earth. She was ready.

Everything that my sister had fought for in life she had overcome. Her biggest battle was forgiving herself. We would talk all the time about letting go of any guilt. She had finally gained a sense of peace and comfort that she had not seen since we were kids. Don't get me wrong; just because I understand life's journey doesn't make the end of life any easier.

After the repast, I was faced with the harsh truth that life moves on without mercy. Time waits for no one. Family and friends will revert back to their normal lives, while you are left to deal with the painful truth that your loved one is no longer here. The world expects you to continue on, even when it feels impossible. Three days of bereavement leave, and then you're supposed to function as if nothing has changed. Even as a business owner, I was expected to keep up with deadlines, to meet expectations. There was no grace given.

I struggled. Some days, I couldn't get out of bed. Mail piled up, unread. My home looked unkempt. Even when I woke up feeling like I could make the day count, the motivation would slip away. I found myself isolating and withdrawing from people. I had to face the fact that depression and grief doesn't care about titles or careers.

As a therapist, I'm used to helping others find their way out of dark places, but I wasn't immune to needing the very same support and strategies. It was humbling to admit that even the "Therapist and Strong Friend"- the person who always made people feel better, needed to apply the tools that she so often recommended to others. In my own journey, I realized that strength isn't about never falling apart—it's about giving yourself permission to feel, to break, and then to rebuild.

Grief: A Journey Through Shadows

During this time, I came face to face with grief's complex, unpredictable nature. Grief is not something you move through in a straight line. I could only wish it was that simple. In fact, psychiatrist Elisabeth Kübler-Ross developed the Five Stages of Grief—denial, anger, bargaining, depression, and acceptance. It's a helpful framework, but it's important to know that you can move between stages at any time, and sometimes, you can feel more than one stage at once.

For me, it was a constant tug-of-war between anger and depression. I felt the weight of the world on my shoulders. Denial wasn't an option—reality was too painful to escape. But bargaining? That showed up in my prayers, in my conversations with God, hoping for a way to make sense of it all.

Grief isn't something you just "get over." It's something you learn to live with, to carry. The goal isn't to erase the pain, but to find ways to coexist with it.

The Path to Healing: Embracing Each Step

The turning point was acknowledging that I was stuck. Depression had taken hold, and I had to make the choice to push myself toward healing. Getting to a place where I could even think about healing wasn't easy. At first, I was paralyzed by the weight of my grief, sinking deeper into isolation and anger. There were days when I felt completely lost, unsure if I'd ever find my way out of the darkness. I had all the tools as a therapist, but using them for myself felt impossible. I was battling my own expectations, as if admitting I was struggling would somehow make me weak. It took time—time to accept that my grief was valid and that I didn't have to be strong all the time. It wasn't until I gave myself permission to be vulnerable that I could finally start putting those healing steps into practice.

The practical steps came slowly, but I knew that I had to take them in order to heal:

1. Acknowledge the Pain: This was the first and hardest step. I had to allow myself to truly feel the hurt, to sit with it, rather than trying to avoid or numb it.

2. Surround Yourself with Support: I learned the importance of leaning on people who understood—whether through therapy, family, or trusted friends. Sometimes, it meant seeking out a professional who could hold space for my grief in a way others couldn't.

3. Small Steps Forward: Healing doesn't come from one grand gesture; it's built on small, intentional actions. Getting out of bed, getting dressed, going for a walk—these steps matter. These actions reminded me that I was still living, still capable of moving forward, even when it felt impossible.

Evidence-Based Grief Coping Strategies

During this process, I leaned on strategies I knew could help. I had moments where it felt useless but I knew consistency was important. Some of the strategies that helped me cope were: Cognitive Behavioral Therapy (CBT), which is one of the most effective methods for managing grief. There were days when the guilt would flood my mind. I'd find myself replaying all the moments I felt I wasn't there for Michelle. The 'what ifs' were relentless. What if I had called more? What if I had spent more time with her? It was easy to spiral into these thoughts, but I knew I needed to challenge them. Instead of allowing myself to be overwhelmed by the endless "what ifs" and guilt that grief often brings, I focused on reframing those negative thought patterns. I practiced recognizing the love and great times I had with my sister, rather than dwelling on regrets or missed moments. Using CBT techniques, I began questioning the validity of those negative thoughts. Had I really not been there for her? I reminded myself of the times we laughed together, the late-night phone calls, the support I gave during her hardest moments. Slowly, I began to shift the narrative. I couldn't change the past, but I could recognize the love I had shown her throughout her life. Reframing those thoughts didn't erase the pain, but it allowed me to hold space for both my grief and my love for her without being consumed by guilt.

Journaling

Writing had always been a source of release for me, but in the depths of my grief, I had stopped. Eventually, I returned to it, allowing the pen to become my outlet. One night, when the weight of grief felt unbearable, I picked up my journal after avoiding it for weeks. At first, the words came slowly—disjointed sentences filled with anger, sadness, and regret. But the more I wrote, the more I felt like I was releasing some of the heaviness inside me. I wrote about the moments we shared, about the memories that brought both joy and pain. I even wrote letters to Michelle, telling her all the things I wished I could say. Journaling became a way for me to process the messiness of my emotions. It was like having a conversation with myself, one that allowed me to make sense of the chaos swirling in my mind. And in that clarity, I began to see a path forward.

I journaled everything—the anger, the sadness, the guilt, and even the glimmers of hope that I sometimes felt. Journaling gave me a place to lay down the weight of my thoughts. It was like talking to a trusted friend who would never interrupt or judge. As the pages filled up, I realized that this was more than just an emotional release; it was a way for me to process and make sense of everything that had happened. Studies have shown that journaling helps individuals manage their emotions and improve mental clarity, and I could feel that clarity slowly returning. It gave me a sense of control, even when life felt uncontrollable.

Exercise and Physical Health

I also knew that my emotional state was linked to my physical health. I'd been neglecting my body, gaining weight, and feeling sluggish, which only deepened my sense of helplessness. The thought of working out felt daunting at first, but I reminded myself that it didn't have to be anything major. I started small, with light stretches or a short walk around the block. The fresh air and movement helped me clear my mind, even if just for a little while. There's a lot of research that shows regular exercise improves mood and reduces symptoms of depression, and though I wasn't looking for a miracle, I did notice a difference.

Slowly, my energy levels increased, and I felt a little more in control of my life again.

Eating Healthier

Another step toward healing was taking better care of what I put into my body. Grief had driven me to emotional eating, and I'd found temporary comfort in unhealthy foods. But as I began to gain a bit more energy from my walks, I realized that food was another area where I could make positive changes. I focused on nourishing my body, rather than feeding my emotions. Eating healthier meals wasn't about fixing everything, but it was about giving myself the strength I needed to keep going, day by day. Practicing What I Preach: Coping as a Therapist.

Being a therapist during this time felt like both a blessing and a curse. On one hand, I knew the tools, the frameworks, and the theories that could help me manage my grief. I'd spent years teaching clients how to cope with loss, depression, and trauma. But now, I was the one in need, and that knowledge sometimes felt like a burden. There was this pressure both from myself and others to 'know better,' to handle my grief with grace because of my profession. People expected me to be strong, to hold it together. But grief doesn't care about degrees or titles, and it doesn't give therapists a free pass. I found myself battling the very expectations I had set for myself as a professional.

Admitting that I needed help felt like a failure at first. How could I, someone who helps others, not help myself? But grief stripped away that facade. I had to accept that being a therapist didn't mean I had to have all the answers, especially when it came to my own pain. It was humbling, and in that humility, I found a new sense of compassion for myself and for others. Now, when I sit with clients who are grieving, I understand their pain on a much deeper level. I no longer see my role as 'fixing' them, but rather walking alongside them in their journey, just as I've had to walk my own.

Finding My Peace: Learning to Live with Loss

As the days turned into weeks and then months, I began to recognize something powerful: grief had changed me, but it hadn't destroyed me. Grief is a journey, and while it never truly ends, it can lead to new growth and understanding. As I continued to move through my grief, I began to notice something shift inside of me. The pain was still there, but alongside it was something new—a deeper sense of purpose. In psychology, this phenomenon is known as Post-Traumatic Growth (PTG). It's the idea that, through immense suffering, we can experience personal growth in ways we never imagined. It doesn't mean the loss was any less painful or that the grief has gone away. But I found myself changed by it. I became more compassionate, not just toward others, but toward myself. I started seeing life differently, appreciating the small moments with loved ones in a way I hadn't before. My priorities shifted. What once felt urgent and important no longer held the same weight. Instead, I focused on what truly mattered—connection, purpose, and authenticity.

Michelle's death has shaped me, not just as a sister, but as a person. I am still learning how to carry this loss, but I also see how it has deepened my capacity for empathy, resilience, and love. PTG doesn't erase the pain, but it gives the pain meaning, transforming it into something that can lead to growth.
For me, that growth is still happening. I'm still learning how to live with the loss, but I've found ways to carry it with grace, to honor my sister by moving forward with my own life.

Conclusion: Hope Amidst Grief

The hole in my heart will always be there, but it doesn't have to stop me from living. I carry Michelle with me in everything I do.

The lessons I've learned in this journey of grief have taught me that healing isn't about moving on, it's about moving forward, finding ways to integrate the loss into who you are and who you're becoming.

For anyone walking through grief, know this: there's no right way to do it. It's messy, unpredictable, and deeply personal. But there are tools and strategies that can help you navigate the darkest days. The pain doesn't disappear, but over time, you'll learn to live with it, and maybe even grow from it. Healing isn't about grand gestures; it's the small, seemingly insignificant actions that make the difference. Getting out of bed when all I wanted to do was hide under the covers. Putting on clothes and brushing my hair, even when it felt pointless. Taking a short walk, feeling the sun on my face, and breathing in the fresh air. These small steps reminded me that I was still living. It wasn't about 'getting over' my grief, it was about learning to coexist with it.

As a therapist, I'd often ask myself, 'What would I recommend to a client in this situation?' Then, I'd try to practice what I preached. It wasn't always easy, and some days I couldn't follow through. But on other days, I could. And those were the days I began to feel like maybe, just maybe, I could make it through.
Each of these small steps, while simple on their own, collectively helped pull me out of the darkest place I'd ever been. It wasn't an overnight transformation, and even now, I have days where the grief feels as fresh as it did the moment I answered that phone call. But the tools—the framework I followed, the evidence-based strategies I practiced—helped me find my way back to myself. The emptiness I feel will always be a part of me, but I'm learning to carry it with grace, and to move forward with my life while honoring Michelle's memory.

Healing isn't a destination; it's a journey - one that requires patience and constant work. Grief will always be part of my story, but it doesn't define the whole of me. And as I continue to navigate this path, I'm grateful for the lessons it has taught me, lessons I now use to help others find their way through the darkness.

Reflecting on Michelle's life and the peace she found, I realized that peace wasn't something distant and unattainable. It was something I could choose to create, even in the midst of my pain. Michelle fought so hard in life, and in the end, she found her peace. Now, it's my turn to find mine.

Grief is a journey with no real end, but through that journey, I've discovered that healing is not about erasing the memories or escaping the sadness. It's about honoring the person you've lost by living the life they would want for you, one filled with purpose, joy, and authenticity. Each day, I remind myself that I'm still here, and while the weight of grief may never fully disappear, I'm learning to carry it differently.

No matter how heavy your grief feels, you are not alone. Healing is messy and unpredictable, but it is possible. And just like I tell my clients, you have the strength inside you to face even the darkest moments. It's not about being strong every second of the day, it's about taking small steps, one at a time, toward the life you deserve.

Michelle's Legacy: Honoring Her Memory

Michelle may be gone, but her spirit and the lessons she taught me live on. In finding my own peace. Michelle was always so proud of my accomplishments as her little sister. She bragged about my business as if it was hers. I honor her every day by showing up in my business and supporting her children in their endeavors. It's in those moments when I reach a career goal, show up for her children, laugh with them, and support them that I feel her presence most, and that's how I continue to honor her memory.

REFLECTIONS

How has grief shaped your perspective on life and relationships?

Reflect on a time when you had to balance personal loss with professional responsibilities. How did you navigate that duality?

What small, intentional steps can you take to move forward in your own journey through grief?

Yvonne Sailor- Walker, LPC

From Early Exposure to Empowerment: My Mental Health Journey

Yvonne Sailor- Walker, LPC

From Early Exposure to Empowerment: My Mental Health Journey

"I can do all things through Christ who strengthens me" - Philippians 4:13 (NKJV)

Mental health has never been the topic of discussion in our home or within our black community growing up. Although it was there and we were often exposed to mental health whether with direct family members or someone associated with our families, it was never talked about or even acknowledged.

My mother has struggled with her addiction for as long as I can remember. Most of the time when she would act out at family functions, family members would say, "Oh well, everyone has one in the family, or she was just called plain ol' "crazy." I would hear stories about my mother when she was a teenager and instances where she would have weird behaviors or would lash out. I can also recall my mother's bizarre stories about how she would hear voices or sounds that no one else would hear. While an undergrad, I studied psychology. I learned more about mental health and human behaviors, and many sounded familiar as I think back to my mother. I later found out that my mother did struggle with what we call mental health, and her diagnosis was Schizophrenia. My mother, like many others in the community, was told by the church that she was battling a demon and that she just needed to "pray about it."

As a young child, her actions and behaviors were embarrassing and caused me to struggle with fear and anxiety. I became upset at what people would say about her because I loved my mother dearly. However, I said that I would never want to be like my mother because she struggled and was so isolated from everyone, even her children. My siblings and I struggled as children and because of our mother's mental illness, we had to grow up without her. We were separated and left to put the pieces together on our own as it pertained to our mother's mental illness and diagnosis.

As I began to educate myself and learn more about schizophrenia, what it was, and how it affected people's moods, behaviors, thoughts, psychology, and speech, it was as if my mother was being described through text. I saw and experienced the impact that the disorder had on me and my siblings, but most importantly, I watched how it impacted my mother's own life. I understood her substance abuse and how she self-medicated to cope with a lot of her struggles and losses. She had to cope with the loss of her career, her home, her relationships with friends, and family, and the loss of her children.

My mother was my very first experience and exposure to mental health and the direct impact that it has on the individual and the family. My mother also showed me that there is truly life beyond diagnosis. Although it was not easy, it came with a lot of setbacks and backlash from people within the family and community, my mother was resilient. She was able to get herself together in the best way she could. She worked hard to reestablish her living situation by getting trained in taxes and business management, and later opened her store. She was the most persevering and resilient person I have ever known. She was a true fighter and will forever be my hero. She did not allow her diagnosis to break her and although she lost so much, she worked hard to pull herself together and live life until her passing in 2017. I never would have thought that my mother's experiences and her own resiliency would later encourage and motivate me during the most challenging time in my life.

Surviving My Diagnosis: A Life Reclaimed.

I thought I had a hold on life, but life had me in a chokehold. I had no idea that it was eating me up at my very core. I didn't realize the impact that my childhood trauma had on me. I was struggling and drowning and didn't even know it. I was destroying relationships with the very people that I held near and dear to me from my children to my husband. I prayed that I wouldn't end up like my own mother and lose everything due to mental illness, but my life was unraveling and I was becoming just what I didn't want to be; at least that's what I thought.

In 2012, I experienced my very first panic attack. At the time I thought it was a heart attack. I was rushed to the nearest hospital thinking this was it; I was going to die. After arriving at the hospital barely able to breathe, speak, or move, I remember them running numerous tests and blood work to come back with a clean bill of health. I was confused as I knew what I was experiencing was not normal, so what did they mean I was ok? This was the very first time I was ever told that I was having what was known as a panic attack - panic attack, what is that? So many thoughts ran through my mind. I asked myself what does this mean, will I need surgery, does this mean I have some underlying health issues? I was so lost and confused. If I was told I was having a heart attack that would have made more sense to me. I didn't understand how my mental health could cause such a physical response within my body; it was all so foreign to me. Little did I know this was just the beginning of a long, terrifying, isolating and confusing time that I was about to encounter. But I also didn't know how this devastation was going to turn into the very thing that changed my life for the better.

My panic attacks turned into me being diagnosed with anxiety, panic disorder, and depression by my primary care physician. I was told that I needed to see a therapist. A therapist - what? No way was I crazy; only crazy folks saw therapists. I've been around too many crazy folks in my life to know what crazy was and that wasn't me. I thought to myself, "I'm not on drugs and I have a home and a family. Crazy people I know don't have all of this, so no, I'm not crazy and I don't need a therapist.

I began to have panic attacks every day, in fact, multiple times a day at the most random times. Frequent trips to the emergency room became regular to me, as I was searching for some kind of diagnosis that made sense to me. I was afraid of dying in my sleep, so I didn't sleep. I didn't drive for over a year as I was afraid of having a panic attack and dying on the road. I was afraid of drowning, so I didn't take baths. I stayed isolated in the house and lost my job as I became unreliable to the agency. My world was crumbling around me. I was once a "supermom" who now required so much help from my husband and family.

I felt as if I was failing, so I turned to God. I've always been told that I should pray about my struggles, so when I went to the elders of the church and my pastor, I was told what I've always been told. I have a demon and I needed to pray for it, so that's just what I did. Prayer and reading my bible was done more than I would eat food or drink water. My life revolved around it as I was hopeful that God was going to cast out this demon that was taking over my mind and body. I realized I couldn't do it on my own, so I buried myself in the church. I changed the way I dressed from pants to skirts, no makeup and I went to church 5-6 days a week. Nothing else mattered; I needed God to free me from this.

As I continued to struggle, no one around understood what I was going through because they saw this healthy-looking body, woman, and mother. To them there was no real logical explanation to what I was going through as they too struggled to identify, connect and understand mental health, what it was or how it could impact your life. It made no sense and it was all too frustrating to me. It caused so much strain, especially in my marriage. I wasn't being "lazy" or a "bad" mother or wife; I was really struggling in silence, and was in such a lonely and isolating place. All I had was prayer. I found myself up at the altar several times a week crying out with my face to the earth crying out to God and didn't care who was watching. I needed to totally surrender to God to experience a supernatural experience that I only knew and had faith that God could provide. I expected God to come change me right there at the altar. I wanted him to send angels to lift me up and to change me forever. I cried out as the Elders of the church told me to, asking God to take "IT" away from me. I pleaded, "God, I need you to take "IT" from me, I can't take "IT" anymore. Please God, please God, please God." This became my daily mantra.

As I continued to struggle, my faith began to waver. I didn't understand why I was still struggling with "IT." There were times I thought about ending my life because I felt this would be the only way to have peace, but I knew it was God who wouldn't allow me to go through with it. I continued to pray, fast, and stayed in my word expecting a supernatural deliverance and change. As I grew closer to God, I began to feel better; however, when I made it home, I began to experience those feelings and thoughts again. I couldn't wait to get back to church where I could have that temporary experience of normalcy.

One day at the altar, my life changed in a way that I could never imagine; I heard a very subtle and peaceful voice say, "Try therapy." It was in the middle of service and I heard God's voice speaking to me. I said, "Therapy- why would I go to therapy when God you are all I need." I was obedient and didn't share this with anyone aside from my husband. I called my insurance company and found an amazing Christian therapist who changed my life.

How Faith and Therapy Became My Salvation

In my first therapy session, I was hesitant and didn't know what to expect. I didn't know what questions to ask or where to begin. I remember telling her briefly why I was there, however, I only had faith in God, not in the therapeutic process. Her response to my ignorance will always resonate with me. She said, "Did you ever think that it was God that sent you to therapy? He has good reasons why he sent you." She also said, "Ok, you trust God so trust in his plans for you, including therapy." I instantly became relaxed and was so grateful for this lady. Not only was she a therapist but she was a Christian therapist who looked like me; it was a win-win for me. So, I was invested from this point on. Little did I know, I was about to embark on a life-changing experience which would completely change the trajectory of my entire life, from my thinking to my overall outcome in life.

Therapy allowed me to be open about my past. I became educated in what trauma was as well as the mental, physical, and emotional impacts it had on my life. I was given a better understanding of my diagnosis and the impact it was having on me which led to my panic attacks. In the meantime, while I was working through my past trauma, I learned healthy coping skills to manage my stress and panic attacks. The most impactful thing that I learned in therapy was my "IT." I often prayed and asked God to take "IT" away, but what was "IT?" What was I struggling with and needed God's deliverance? God wants us to pray intentionally and precisely in order to have a deeper and more meaningful connection with him. 1 Thessalonians 5:17 instructs us to pray purposefully - to pray always. Through therapy, God revealed to me exactly what I needed to pray for, which was my "IT." "IT" was the trauma that was keeping me bound and not allowing me to grow. "IT" was my insecurities as a woman, mother, and wife which derived from my childhood. "It" was those people that hurt me, that I could not forgive or forget. "IT" was the lack of confidence and motivation that I had as a woman of God because I felt less than. Why? Because of what I was told as a child.

As I began to discover what "IT" was, my prayer changed. When I went to the altar, I came with a new level of confidence. I was deliberate and intentional with my prayer. I prayed for forgiveness, as I forgave others that hurt me. I prayed over my insecurities and cast my burdens unto God.The Bible says, "Cast thy burden unto the Lord, and he shall sustain thee: he shall never suffer the righteous to be moved" (King James Version Psalm 5:22). My walk, talk, and look began to change. God changed me in the blink of an eye. Who would have thought that through my broken and most vulnerable place of my adult life, God would change that young, broken, and damaged child? One of my favorite scriptures is "For as the body without the spirit is dead, so faith without works is dead also" (King James Version 2:14-26). God gave me this scripture during my 3 AM war (prayer) hours. He told me clearly that I exercised my Faith by believing in the word of God, going to church and praying, but my "works" was therapy which allowed me to do the work necessary for complete healing and restoration. As a result, my work and my faith didn't result in my physical, spiritual, or emotional death. I am alive and I owe it all to my Lord and Savior Jesus Christ.

My Praise is Different

Today my praise is different. When I rejoice and cry out, people around me don't understand, but I know my praise is rejoicing in the heavens and causing the Devil to tremble. What the Devil intended for my bad, God turned around for my good. God said that I would not be what people spoke over my life as a child; I would be great and grow up to do wonderful things. I've created you in my image and planted seeds in you far before you reached the earth. Those seeds will be manifested, and greatness will overtake your life. This is what God spoke to me.

I recognize that healing is a process, forgiveness is a choice and a process, and I choose to forgive those who tried to hurt me physically, mentally, and emotionally. God turned my test into a testimony, and I thank him for the many opportunities to share it with the world. Stay encouraged no matter what the storm looks like; I know that life isn't easy and there are times when many of us want to give up, but I am a living testimony to hold on. I am not who I was told I would be or what statistics said I would be. Statistics said that because my mother and father were addicts, I would likely be an addict, and because marriages or relationships didn't last in my family, mine was likely to end in divorce. Statistics would show that if you grew up in a single-parent home or in foster care, your children would most likely live in a single parent home.

Although my life hasn't been perfect, I have some battle wounds, but I'm standing strong. I have a beautiful family, and I'm striving daily to be the best wife and mother that I can be. I pursued my degree in Counseling Psychology, and I am now the proud owner and CEO of Radiant Life Psychotherapy LLC. I work with families and individuals as a Christian therapist. I thank God because I can naturally be empathetic to my client, as we are taught in grad school that empathy is the highest level of emotional regard that we can show another human being.

I have shared my testimony to encourage clients in their toughest times. I'm able to share with them about the wonderful God that we serve and how he can change their lives through prayer and his word. I am a therapist who works with individuals and couples by creating real change within themselves and their relationships through the power of prayer and therapy. I thank God for allowing me to be his vessel. I know and trust that he only gives his toughest battles to his strongest soldiers. I thank God for my mother and her experiences because it was often my motivation to keep pressing forward. I watched her transform all while battling her mental illness. I would thank God that I had a mother that was strong and resilient, and I was created with the strength that she had within her. "I am my mother's child." I once cursed the very thought of being like my mother because of the negative perception that I had about mental illness. I was made to believe that those who struggled with mental illness would be subject to a death sentence, and that those who struggled with it would lose everything and turn to drugs. But God showed me something different when it came to my struggle. He allowed me to look beyond my mother's diagnosis and see her strength and resiliency, and for that I am forever grateful for her being my mother.

Living Boldly Beyond the Diagnosis

There is life beyond the diagnosis and I'm a living witness. I thought my diagnosis was the end for me - I was going to live and die with depression and anxiety disorder. I thought it was going to ruin and control the rest of my life, but God had other plans. Little did I know that God was, in fact, going to use my diagnosis to completely heal and set me free. I can stand confidently today and say that I thank God for my diagnosis. Was it hard? Yes. Did I want to give up? Yes. I even turned to medication to help me through my most difficult days and I thank God for the journey.

Although every day isn't perfect, I'm going to be honest and transparent. Do I still struggle with panic attacks? Absolutely, but I'm aware of what it is and I utilize my coping skills to help me through it. I experience anxiety, but it pushes me harder to keep going and continue to do more. I can now freely pour into myself and prioritize my mental health which is so important for us to do. I do periodic check-ins with myself and when I feel as if I'm getting too overwhelmed, I take a step back, ask for help, and give myself GRACE. Through my own diagnosis and healing journey, I can walk into my true purpose and true self as a therapist, mom, wife, and friend.

One of my favorite songs to listen to is "People" by Jonathan McReynolds. Listening to this song has been so liberating for me. One of the verses is "People, people when you said you could heal me from many things, did you mean people, people, deliver me, cause I can't point 'me out I won't say their names, I don't know the damage, or which one to blame it's just people, people deliver me..." This song really speaks to me as a reminder of the impact that people can have on you - from loved ones to strangers, people constantly impact us. We can allow the things that people say to destroy, break, and create us, or we can pray and ask God to deliver us from these people and the things that they've done to us. It's not about me calling out these people and putting them on blast as they know who they are and what they have done. I know and God knows.

By asking God to deliver me, I can truly heal and so can you. My goal is to encourage those within our community to prioritize their mental health, seek help, and start their healing journey today. There is healing beyond the diagnosis. YOU must make the choice to change. Through prayer and therapy, change can happen just as it did for me. I made the choice to live beyond my diagnosis and it was the best decision that I made. We are all given the freedom of choice. What will you choose today?

Yes, I am Yvonne Sailor-Walker, Licensed Professional Counselor, diagnosed at the age of twenty-seven with anxiety, depression, and panic disorder. I've taken medication, sought therapy, and allowed God to change my entire life. I am living my best life, and so can you!!!

REFLECTIONS

Reflect on a time when you experienced resilience in the face of adversity. How did that experience shape your current path?

How has your understanding of mental health evolved through your personal or professional journey?

If you could offer advice to your younger self, what would you say about overcoming challenges and embracing growth?

Tawanna Marie Woolfolk, LCSW

Standing My Sacred Ground: A Journey of Healing and Purpose

Tawanna Marie Woolfolk, LCSW

Standing My Sacred Ground: A Journey of Healing and Purpose

Who benefits from your shrinking? Who can be trusted as you expand? We need one another to see our faces clearly. Find safe company for the journey. - Cole Arthur Riley

My journey is nothing short of extraordinary. It is a testament to human resilience and the profound impact of finding purpose amid the darkest of circumstances. With over two decades of clinical experience, specializing in complex trauma treatment and integrated wellness services, I have become a beacon of hope for many. As a licensed clinical social worker with a MSW from Smith College School for Social Work, certified as an EMDR therapist, Trauma Professional, and Grief Specialist, I have dedicated my life to planting mustard seeds of hope and faith through clinical work, public speaking, training, education, supervision, and consultation. But my journey to this point is a story that begins with immense hardship and ends in tremendous triumph.

Surviving Trauma: The Foundation of My Strength

My early years were marked by unimaginable challenges. I grew up in the foster care system after suffering from malnutrition, educational neglect, and sexual and physical trauma. The basic necessities that many take for granted were luxuries to me. I vividly recall the times I drank out of toilets and ate from trash cans, merely to survive. Starting kindergarten at the age of eight, I was significantly behind my peers, both academically and socially. Despite these early adversities, I always had an intuitive sense about the right people to trust and guide me toward resilience. This innate wisdom eventually led me to a path of healing and helping others heal. But before I could help others, I had to find my own way.

The nights were often the hardest. I remember lying awake, the weight of silence pressing down on me, wondering if I would ever escape the cycle of abuse and neglect. This was when my battle with annihilation anxiety began to take root. According to Hartmann (2020), annihilation anxiety involves the fear of total destruction and nonexistence, often stemming from early trauma. For me, this manifested as a persistent, gnawing fear that I was not meant to exist, that my life was a mistake. This anxiety was compounded by the constant instability and uncertainty in my life (Kalsched, 2013).

I learned early on that hope was a fragile thing, easily shattered by the harsh realities of my life. The pervasive sense of not belonging, of being an outsider, haunted me. I often felt like a ghost, drifting through life unnoticed and unloved. This sense of invisibility is a common experience among those with annihilation anxiety, as they struggle to find a sense of self-worth and belonging (Laing, 1960). Yet, in those quiet, lonely moments, a spark of determination began to grow within me.

The Power of Kindness: Discovering Hope

School was particularly challenging. Starting kindergarten at eight meant I was always playing catch-up. My peers were far ahead academically and socially, and I often felt like I was drowning. The fear of failure was ever-present, feeding my annihilation anxiety. The constant reminders of my inadequacies made it difficult to form meaningful relationships or feel a sense of achievement. According to Winnicott (1960), children who experience such profound early trauma often struggle with feelings of worthlessness and the fear that their very existence is under threat.

Despite these overwhelming challenges, I found solace in small victories and the rare moments of kindness from teachers and mentors who recognized my potential. These individuals became lifelines, helping me to navigate the turbulent waters of my early years. They saw something in me that I struggled to see in myself—a spark of resilience, a glimmer of hope. Their belief in me was like a lifeline, pulling me from the depths of despair.

It was through these relationships that I began to build a sense of self-worth and purpose. I learned to trust my intuition and to seek out people who would support and guide me. This journey was not easy, but it was essential for my healing. Over time, I began to transform my pain into a source of strength. My experiences became the foundation upon which I would build my career in social work, helping others who had faced similar traumas.

Today, I look back on those early years not with regret, but with a sense of gratitude for the lessons they taught me. Annihilation anxiety no longer defines me; instead, it has become a part of my story, a testament to my resilience and determination to not just survive, but to thrive.

My sense of empowerment around taking risks and internalizing all nuances of myself has been deeply impacted by the complex trauma and neurodivergence that have shaped my life. Annihilation anxiety, a profound and pervasive sense of existential threat, has been a formidable challenge in my journey toward self-empowerment and holistic self-understanding. The basic danger involved in annihilation anxiety is a threat to psychic survival, experienced as a present menace or an anticipation of imminent catastrophe (Hartmann, 2020). This experience encompasses fantasies and feelings of helplessness in the face of inner and outer dangers against which I have felt powerless to take protective or constructive action.

I endured malnutrition, educational neglect, and sexual and physical trauma before transitioning into the foster care system. These early experiences left me feeling vulnerable and defenseless, unable to regulate my emotions or environment. Freud's 1926 view of a traumatic situation describes this well: a person faced with a quantity of stimulation they cannot discharge or master, leading to a failure of self-regulation (Freud, 1926). For me, this meant that the constant barrage of fear, pain, and uncertainty overwhelmed my capacity to cope, resulting in a pervasive sense of helplessness and a deep-seated fear of annihilation.

Annihilation anxiety has many facets, often manifesting as fears of being overwhelmed, destroyed, abandoned, or going insane (Winnicott, 1960). These fears have haunted me, shaping my thoughts, behaviors, and emotional responses. The terror of being consumed by these anxieties made it difficult to take risks or embrace my neurodivergent identity fully. I feared that any misstep, any vulnerability, could lead to a catastrophic unraveling of my already fragile psyche.

Taking risks has always been a daunting prospect for me. The prospect of failure or rejection would trigger my annihilation anxieties, filling me with an overwhelming sense of dread. I feared that taking a risk and failing would confirm my deepest fears: that I was fundamentally unworthy and incapable of success. This fear of failure was compounded by my neurodivergence, which often made me feel different and misunderstood. The societal pressures to conform and the stigma associated with neurodivergence intensified my anxieties, making it even harder to step out of my comfort zone.

Internalizing all nuances of myself, including my neurodivergence, has been equally challenging. Annihilation anxiety can lead to a fragmented sense of self, where parts of one's identity are disowned or hidden to avoid the perceived threat of annihilation (Kalsched, 2013). For a long time, I struggled to accept and embrace my neurodivergent traits, fearing that they would make me more vulnerable to rejection and abandonment. This self-rejection further eroded my sense of empowerment, as I felt unable to fully inhabit my own identity. Embracing my neurodivergence has been a transformative aspect of my journey. Recognizing that my unique ways of thinking and perceiving the world are strengths, rather than deficiencies, has empowered me to take risks and pursue my passions with confidence. Celebrating my neurodivergent traits has also allowed me to connect with others who share similar experiences, fostering a sense of community and mutual support.

The journey toward empowerment and self-acceptance has required me to confront and work through these deep-seated anxieties. The combination of somatic attachment focused EMDR (Eye Movement Desensitization Reprocessing Therapy), psychoanalytic therapy, mindfulness therapy and inner child work, have been instrumental in the evolutionary process of my healing. Understanding the roots of my annihilation anxiety and how it manifests in my thoughts and behaviors has helped me develop greater self-awareness and resilience. Therapy has allowed me to explore and integrate the various aspects of my identity, fostering a more cohesive and empowered sense of self.

In therapy, I have learned to recognize and challenge the catastrophic thinking patterns that fuel my annihilation anxieties. These patterns often involve anticipating the worst possible outcomes and feeling utterly helpless in the face of perceived threats (Stern, 2010). By identifying these thought patterns and replacing them with more balanced and realistic perspectives, I have begun to reduce the intensity of my anxieties and build a stronger foundation for taking risks and embracing my neurodivergence.

Developing a supportive network has also been crucial in my journey. Surrounding myself with people who understand and accept my neurodivergent identity has provided a sense of safety and belonging that counters my fears of rejection and abandonment. This support has encouraged me to take risks and explore new possibilities, knowing that I have a safety net to catch me if I fall and if I fail.

Mindfulness and self-compassion practices have further aided my empowerment. Learning to be present with my emotions, without judgment, has helped me navigate the intense feelings associated with annihilation anxiety. Practicing self-compassion has allowed me to treat myself with kindness and understanding, rather than harsh criticism, when I struggle or make mistakes. This shift in attitude has made it easier to take risks and internalize all nuances of myself, knowing that I can handle whatever comes my way with grace and resilience.
In conclusion, the impact of annihilation anxiety on my sense

of empowerment and ability to internalize all nuances of myself has been profound. The pervasive fears and feelings of helplessness associated with this anxiety have made taking risks and embracing my neurodivergent identity a daunting challenge. However, through therapy, self-awareness, supportive relationships, and mindfulness practices, I have begun to confront and overcome these anxieties. By recognizing my strengths and embracing all aspects of my identity, I am building a more empowered and resilient self. My journey is a testament to the possibility of growth and healing, even in the face of deep-seated fears and trauma.

Defining Meaning in Suffering

The turning point in my life came in the third grade when I discovered Viktor E. Frankl's book, Man's Search for Meaning. Up until that time, I had been plagued by questions about my existence. Why was I alive? How had I survived such horrific conditions? Frankl's words became a survival guide for me. His exploration of finding meaning through suffering resonated deeply with me. It was as though Frankl had handed me a roadmap, filled with mustard seeds of hope that I could cling to until I found my purpose.

Frankl's insights into the human condition and the quest for meaning gave me a new perspective on my own suffering. I began to see my experiences not just as a series of painful events, but as part of a larger journey toward finding my purpose. This shift in perspective was transformative. For the first time, I felt a sense of hope that transcended my immediate circumstances. I began to believe that there was a reason for my existence, a reason that went beyond the pain I had endured.

Overcoming the Past

My early aspirations did not include becoming a therapist. I dreamt of a career in the culinary arts, fine arts, cosmetology, or massage therapy. These fields offered a creative outlet and a way to escape the pain of my past. However, my journey would take an unexpected turn that would lead me to discover my true calling.

After traveling around the world and spending six months in Australia, I began to see social work as a viable path. Up until that point, two influential people in my life had seen my potential as a social worker. One even envisioned me at Smith College School for Social Work. Encouraged by their belief in me, I decided to apply to Smith College. With the support of my international team of peers, I put together my application package and awaited the response.

My travels opened my eyes to the vastness of the world and the myriad of possibilities that lay before me. Each new place I visited, each new person I met, contributed to my growing sense of self and my understanding of the human condition. I realized that my past did not have to define my future, that I had the power to shape my own destiny. The idea of becoming a social worker began to take root, fueled by my desire to help others who had experienced trauma and hardship.

From Doubt to Acceptance

When I was called for an interview at Smith College, I was met with skepticism. I was told that I was too young and not established enough to represent their graduate school. The interviewer's words stung, but my resolve was unshakable. I slammed my hand on the desk and asserted that I was meant to be there. My determination paid off; I was one of five students accepted straight out of college.

This acceptance was a pivotal moment in my life. It validated my belief in myself and set me on a path that would lead to a remarkable career. I immersed myself in my studies at Smith College, determined to make the most of the opportunity I had fought so hard to secure.

During my time at Smith College, I encountered numerous challenges. The rigorous academic environment was demanding, and I often felt the weight of my past bearing down on me. Yet, I remained steadfast in my commitment to my studies. I knew that my success would not only be a personal triumph but also a beacon of hope for others who had faced similar adversities.

The Art of Healing

Over the next 20 years, my career flourished. I realized that social work was not just a profession for me; it was an art and a science. I blended hospitality with clinical expertise, leading by example and demonstrating an abundance of love and trust in my clients' ability to heal. My approach was masterful and creative, deeply rooted in the belief that everyone has the potential to overcome their trauma and thrive.

At Sacred Ground Institute, LLC, I created a sanctuary for healing. My clients found solace in my empathetic and intuitive approach. I understood their pain because I had lived it. My journey from a malnourished, neglected child to a successful therapist and CEO was a beacon of hope for those I served. My life's work was a testament to the power of resilience and the importance of finding meaning in the face of suffering.

My approach to therapy was deeply influenced by my own experiences. I knew firsthand the importance of feeling seen and heard, of having someone believe in your potential. I worked tirelessly to create a space where my clients could feel safe and supported, where they could begin their own journeys of healing and self-discovery. My clients often spoke of the profound impact I had on their lives, of how I helped them find hope and meaning amid their struggles.

For over 40 years, I struggled with the belief that I was not meant to exist and with annihilation anxiety. I questioned why I had been born and what my purpose was. It was not until I underwent the deepest of my own healing that I truly found the answers. This profound personal transformation was the catalyst for my decision to share my story and apply for opportunities that would amplify my impact.

My healing journey was multifaceted. It involved confronting my past traumas, embracing my identity, and finding strength in my vulnerabilities. Through therapy, self-reflection, and the unwavering support of trusted individuals, I began to see myself in a new light. I realized that my experiences, no matter how painful, had shaped me into the person I was meant to be. The process of healing was not easy. It required me to face the darkest parts of my past, to relive the pain and trauma I had endured. But with each step, I grew stronger. I learned to forgive myself and others, to let go of the anger and resentment that had been weighing me down. I discovered a new sense of purpose, one that was rooted in my desire to help others heal and find meaning in their own lives.

Embracing My Purpose

My decision to apply for new opportunities was driven by a

newfound sense of purpose. I was tired of hiding and ready to embrace my existence fully. I knew that my story could inspire others to overcome their own challenges and find meaning in their lives. I believed that I was a sure bet, destined to make a difference in the world.

This anthology chapter is a declaration of deep belief in myself and my mission. My journey is a powerful narrative of resilience, hope, and the relentless pursuit of meaning. I had transformed my pain into a source of strength and inspiration for others.

As I shared my story with others, I found that my experiences resonated deeply with people from all sociocultural contexts. I received letters and messages from individuals who had been inspired by my journey, who had found hope and strength in my words. I realized that my story had the power to touch lives and create change, and I embraced this role with passion and dedication.

Owning My Impact and Legacy

My life is a testament to the incredible power of resilience and the importance of finding meaning in the face of adversity. From a childhood marked by trauma and neglect to a successful career as a licensed clinical social worker and CEO of Sacred Ground Institute, LLC, my journey is one of hope and transformation. My discovery of Viktor E. Frankl's Man's Search for Meaning was a turning point that provided me with the guidance I needed to navigate my path.

My story is a beacon of hope for those who have experienced trauma and are searching for their purpose beyond their afflictions and diagnoses. It is a reminder that even in the darkest of times, there are mustard seeds of hope that can guide us toward healing and fulfillment. My life's work is dedicated to planting these seeds of hope and faith in others, helping them find their own path to resilience and meaning. I learned early on that hope was a fragile thing, easily shattered by the harsh realities of my life. Yet, in the darkest, quiet, and loneliest moments of my despair, a spark of determination grew within me. I refuse to be defined by my circumstances. I refuse to be broken. I refuse to continue making myself and worth a non-factor. I GET TO stand my sacred ground and own my impact and purpose.

REFLECTIONS

What does standing your ground mean to you, and how do you maintain your sense of purpose in difficult times?

Think about a moment when kindness or a mentor helped guide you through adversity. How did that impact your journey?

How do you nurture and honor your own healing process while supporting others in theirs?

Dr. Tasha N. Rose, LPC

Faith Beyond the Pain: A Journey to Healing and Purpose

Dr. Tasha N. Rose, LPC

Faith Beyond the Pain: A Journey to Healing and Purpose

"For I know the plans I have for you," declares the Lord, "plans to prosper you and not to harm you, plans to give you hope and a future." - Jeremiah 29:11 NIV

Defining Faith: The Foundation of My Journey

When I was invited to participate in an anthology, I was excited, but then my excitement turned into anxiety and worry. I was anxious about what I would share, who would want to read it, and whether God would allow me to expose those who have harmed or helped me throughout my life. I was worried about not being able to write my chapter and ensure that it would be inspirational, interesting, engaging, etc.

Over the next few months, we talked about it briefly, and I was given the book's title; I thought, "How can I tie this into something great?" As a mental health counselor, I am very conscious of how a diagnosis can affect a person's life and future. The Webster's Dictionary defines diagnosis as "the art or act of identifying a disease from its signs and symptoms" (Merriam-Webster, n.d). Although counselors want to be able to identify the cause of the symptoms a client is having, some people are apprehensive about the possibility of being labeled with a diagnosis. Then I thought about how to connect my story to this book title. As I began to ponder what to share, I began to think about how amazing it would be to have an opportunity to share with the world, and the word "FAITH" came to mind. When I think about how I meet with clients daily, how many of them tell me that they have faith and that they will be able to learn to heal while working with me?

I've had faith since I was a little girl. I have always believed that God would elevate and bring me through. Now this doesn't mean I didn't experience trauma, hurts, and pains throughout my life, but I have always had a strong connection with God. Webster's Dictionary says, "Faith is "allegiance to duty or a person: loyalty" (Merriam-Webster, n.d); it also says, "Faith can mean belief and trust in and loyalty to God" (Merriam-Webster, n.d). Both definitions allow us to see that to have faith, you must trust and be loyal. Over my 40-plus years, I have not always been loyal or trustworthy to everyone, but God has always been right here with me. I began to think of my life from when I was a toddler to my adulthood and realized that my story is a story of faith. So, when it was time to actually figure out what I wanted to share, I went to my 24 and 17-year-old daughters for some direction; they both told me I should tell my story and how I have learned to navigate through my pain with FAITH.

To help you understand my story and the way I have learned to process and heal my diagnosis of anxiety and depression, I developed the acronym FAITH. FAITH is forgiveness, accountability, intention, transparency, and healing. You see, as a counselor, I too have dealt with anxiety and depression. There is no cheat code to this, and honestly, if you live in this world, you will have experienced these two cousins (anxiety and depression) together or separately at some point in your lives.

Unspoken Wounds: How Childhood Trauma Shaped My Faith

It was around July 4, 1987. My immediate family and I always did things together with our extended families - my mother's sisters, brothers, and their wives and husbands - and this was no different. On this day, we visited Ocean Beach in New London, CT, about 45-50 minutes from our home in Hartford, CT. I am the youngest daughter of my mom and dad. There I was at the edge of the sand where the sand and the ocean met with my white one-piece; it was a white with red polka dots bathing suit with a red, a white, and a blue bow going vertically down the left side of my body. I had a sand bucket and a shovel going to get some wet sand to make a sandcastle. I went deeper out into the ocean to get more water and that is when I saw it, this colorless, plastic paper flowing little thing in the water.

Guess what? I wanted to touch it. This is where I had my first impactful trauma as a child. It was a jellyfish and because I was curious and nosey, I pulled it right out of the water and it stung me. The burning from the sting sent me running in pure terror to my mother, where I was met with, "I told you not to get into that water-what happened?" There were lots of laughs between the adults. You see, these memories were sketched into my head when I was only six years old. I never understood how this incident shaped me as a young girl or a woman later in my life. Through this incident and its aftermath, I became afraid to get into ocean water and also realized that bad things would happen if I didn't follow directions. This was not my last traumatizing encounter; throughout my childhood, I have had many anxiety-provoking situations that caused me anxiety and depression.

The list goes on; when I was in the third grade, I was prescribed glasses. At the time, I thought these glasses were nice because of the clear, pink frames. But guess what? My lenses were very thick. When I finally wore them to school, the kids were very mean; they called me names and made fun of everything except my clothes. My mom would braid my hair in cornrows going straight back or up in a ponytail; I would be talked about even more because I always had braids when many other girls had their hair out, in ponytails, and other styles. Not being the prettiest girl brought mean and nasty words thrown at me: "You ugly," "You look like a boy," and "If you are a girl, show me." In those moments, I was embarrassed and annoyed; I began thinking of ways to be likable or stop the teasing. I became the "athletic funny girl" and the "loyal and protective friend." These are things that I began to shelter myself from so I could stop being bullied. This didn't always help, but it allowed me to find others who seemed to like me, and I began to feel less anxious.

This is where I also became known as the friend who was always available, the helpful one, and the friend who would stand up for someone in need. These were all mechanisms that allowed me to escape the negative feelings that I had from being bullied. Although I was not the prettiest, I was a likable person, and because I grew up with many boys and was daddy's girl, I enjoyed basketball, football, and whatever else was a physical sport and was pretty good at them. So, because of this, I felt anxious about being a nice, likable person. This made me feel safe because if I was nice and popular to some extent, people wouldn't bother me. This also bred my humorous side; due to my confidence being shattered and the feelings of inadequacies, I became a class clown, leading me to get into trouble at home and school. Not only did I go from being called names for my looks, I also went to being talked about because my dad would come to the school and discipline me when I would get into trouble.

Unveiling the Truth: Living with Anxiety and Depression

This behavior followed me into high school as well. I was so anxious about being talked about or rejected that I used sports and humor to keep me from falling apart. Although it may have looked like I had everything together, I was constantly stressed about the next time I would be talked about. I know you're probably thinking about how this connects; let me help you. I didn't tell you that the jellyfish incident made me feel like I could handle anything, like pain was not supposed to be shown and could be funny. Do you remember how I explained that I ran to my mom for comfort? Do you remember me saying my mother comforted me? No, I said there were questions, ridicule, and then laughter. Well, that's where it started.

Being scared or hurt does not always equate to getting your needs met, so you learn how to navigate through pain the best way you know how. Let me not go too far and say I didn't have loving parents who cared for me and took care of me and my siblings; they did, and they did the best they could. But my parents were not good with being comforting. It was more like, "Go rinse it off," "Be careful because I don't want to have to go to the hospital," and "I don't have money to replace it if you break it." This is what I can remember growing up, which led me to always be extra careful about everything. In turn, this caused me a lot of anxiety as a child and as an adult.

Remember when I said I was diagnosed with depression as well as anxiety? Well, let's talk a little about this. When I was a young girl between the ages of 8-11, I was molested. This didn't happen often, but once is too much. I was also raped during my freshman year in college by a peer and with both, not many knew about it, and I never pursued a consequence due to fear and confusion. I know you may be thinking, "How does this happen?" The truth of the matter is that many people are walking around holding onto things that they may never share, and it is causing them to be dysfunctional. This book is so essential for two reasons: we can help others understand there is life beyond the diagnosis and there is healing in the telling.

I was about 16 when a boy told me I was pretty and he thought I was cool. I was so excited to hear this from someone other than my mother, father, and family. I don't remember my friends telling me I was pretty until later in my adolescence. I also remember catching the eyes of boys in high school because they thought I had a nice body. Now, this made me feel good and since my parents never talked to me about boys or sex, I was like a baby and could not see that the guys who never noticed me were suddenly interested in me. This led me to not make the best choices in relationships. I couldn't see through the lies and deceit; I was just happy to be noticed. I also believe that with my childhood sexual trauma, I learned how to be secretive about things, and if some guy liked me in private, I felt that it was okay, not realizing it was a bad thing.

When I was around 7 or 8 years old, I encountered my first inappropriate touching from an older cousin. However, I didn't think it was wrong since I was close to my cousin because he always made me feel included. I was a "tomboy," so growing up, I spent a lot of time with the boys. The abuse went on for a few years, and then it stopped. I don't think it stopped because I said something because I never did. It stopped because my cousin began dating and no longer needed me, I guess. Although this assault stopped, it continued with another cousin until I was about 12 years old, which led me down a road of depression and false confidence in junior high and high school.

I was voted funniest and class flirt; these are two titles I am not proud of as a healed woman but as an unhealed girl, it was cool. I learned how to hide my emotions by being highly flirtatious and believing that having the attention of males was important. Although I am a pretty happy person now, in high school, I was trying to escape being exposed or not being accepted. I also believe this is how I was vulnerable in college when my peer took advantage of me. Because of the anxiety of wanting to be liked and the depression of not being seen, I thought he liked me due to my lack of judgment and confidence. He made me feel like I was cute and wanted; he was attractive and I said, "Oh, you like me," because I couldn't believe he would like me. Depression and low self-esteem can make you do things that you would be more cautious or wouldn't do if you were thinking with a healthy mind. Due to all I had been holding on to and not addressing, that peer raped me in my room, and it was so disrespectful and embarrassing that I left school after my first semester without telling anyone until years later.

Due to depression, anxiety, and social norms not being addressed, my behaviors continued into my adulthood. I was sad, but I really couldn't tell anyone because everyone looked at me as the happy, confident "Tasha" who wouldn't let anyone hurt her, but the truth was I was in a dark place for a long time. I had my first daughter two weeks before my 19th birthday. I married her dad at 24; we had another daughter one year after our wedding, and I thought I was the happiest and luckiest woman on the earth! That quickly changed once I began doing things that I realized a happy woman wouldn't do. I would hang out with friends more, vacation without my husband, allow men to flirt with me, and I would also flirt back. This was not the behavior of a happily married woman; I don't care how old I was. I was in therapy by now. I enrolled in school and focused on what made me happy. There were times that I would be so unhappy, I wanted to be divorced because I didn't feel wanted or seen by my husband.

My husband was good to me for the most part; however, due to my trauma, I could not see it. I became depressed and did not want to be in a marriage with someone who didn't see me. Don't get me wrong, my husband had done things I was not happy about, such as drinking more than I liked, going out often, coming in the house late, and entertaining others. After a few years of struggling to be a new wife and mother of two children, a full-time student and a full-time employee, I was exhausted. I was diagnosed with General Anxiety and Depression and was given tools to help me learn to navigate them.

I had begun attending church more over the past five to six years and was more connected to God. I started to feel free and empowered. I began to identify with some of the things I had gone through and how they had impacted my life on so many levels and I was ready to start doing the work myself. There are so many things I regret, and one is not knowing about therapy and the effects of it early in my life. I believe if I had been aware and able to seek treatment, I would not have had to deal with so much for so long.

Eventually, I would separate from my husband and ultimately divorce him. This was not an easy decision, and although many, including him, didn't believe I made the best decision, I decided to do so with a clear and healthy mind. I became a much happier and healthier woman for myself. I was a better and more present mother. Don't get me wrong, I still struggled with anxiety, but as a new business owner and mother of two young adults, who wouldn't have anxiety?

The Power of FAITH: A Framework for Healing

During the winter of 2016, I was recently separated and trying to figure things out as a single woman. You see, I had never lived alone and being married, I never really had to worry about much, so this caused some anxiety, therefore, I continued with therapy. I spent a lot of time alone since our children spent most of that year with their dad at his home. I was alone and sometimes I felt sad that I didn't have many people to visit or keep me company. During this time, God revealed many things about me, my past, and what he wanted for me. I prayed and asked God for direction. I was having a regular conversation, like I was talking to myself. I thought I was fine. I thought I was released from what was causing me sadness and anxiety by separating from my husband, but God said he had bigger plans for me. For almost a year, God had me alone most of the time. I had been promoted, and I would travel about an hour and a half to work every day which gave me even more alone time.

I would take the train to and from work and God began speaking to me. He told me I needed to forgive those who hurt me, including myself. I needed to take accountability for the things I have contributed, be intentional about my future, and be transparent and honest with those around me. This needed to happen in order for healing to take place and help to be given. This is where the acronym FAITH was created.

God told me to have faith in him, and I needed to believe and trust that he would get me through everything. Prior to this time alone, I would not have thought that I was insecure, a people pleaser, self-conscious, depressed, angry, and disconnected. Through all the trauma throughout my life, I always thought that I had a handle on things and was in control. And that was the problem; I was in control. I controlled every part of me so that people could not see my flaws. I made sure that I dressed nicely, was put together, my kids were good, and I was educated and had a nice car. I also had an excellent job; it appeared that I had everything. Still, I was so unhappy and miserable, and no one but God could see it. People thought I was just being selfish and inconsiderate of others' feelings. They weren't taking into consideration that I was depressed, anxious, and was falling apart.

You know, sometimes we put ourselves together to hide the pain deep within. This is precisely why I was excited to share a part of my story with you because it's essential to understand that no matter what you look like on the outside, it does not always mean that is what's represented within. God saw me from the inside out because he made me. Sometimes, our parents cannot see the hurt that we may be experiencing because they're human. Being diagnosed with depression and anxiety while being in the mental health field made me feel useless and I did not want to practice.

I didn't want to meet with people and tell them how they should do things because I felt that I was broken. So, in that year of separation from my husband and family, my children had to allow me to get the help that I needed. God was able to talk to me and show me where I needed to be and what I needed to do, which was to believe in him and stand on his word. Not only on his word but to actually use therapy as a tool and use it wisely. Going to therapy does not mean you only go see your therapist daily, weekly or whenever. While going to therapy, you must be dedicated, excited about change, and be open to being uncomfortable in order to heal. Because I wasn't honest with them, I went through three therapists before finding the one that fit best. God sat me down and showed me that I constantly went out looking for services, knowing that I wasn't ready to change. He showed and brought me to my current therapist today. I've been able to not only begin my healing journey with God, but also with a professional in the mental health field to help keep me on track. I only use my faith to heal and get me through dark times, but I use the tools, professionals, and opportunities that God placed before me to get into the space I'm in today.

Living Beyond the Diagnosis: My Purpose Renewed

Today, I continue to use the FAITH acronym to help me stay grounded and connected to God. I have used the skills that God and my therapist have given me, and I use the tools daily to keep me focused and healthy. I also teach others how to live a healthier life using the FAITH acronym, where I teach other women how to use forgiveness, accountability, intention, transparency, and healing to move beyond the diagnosis they have or may be dealing with today.

So when I talk about "beyond the diagnosis," that is what I mean! Once you learn your triggers, how to heal through them, and how to develop new habits, you will be beyond the diagnosis!

REFLECTIONS

How has faith played a role in your healing journey, and how does it continue to shape your decisions?

Reflect on a time when forgiveness was a key to moving forward. What lessons did you learn?

How can you use intention and transparency to foster healing in your relationships and personal life?

Tawana L. Preston, LMSW

The Power of a Motivated Mindset: Turning Struggles into Success

Tawana L. Preston, LMSW

The Power of a Motivated Mindset: Turning Struggles into Success

"I can do all things through Christ which strengtheneth me."- Philippians 4:13 (KJV)

A motivated mindset is the thing that keeps you going. It is the thing that you lean into when you do not know which way to turn. The impact of having a motivated mindset can be the difference between life and death. A motivated mindset is one of the most important tools that an individual needs when trying to figure out their life beyond a diagnosis.

Diagnosis with Dignity

When diagnosing clients, I attempt to deliver the diagnosis with dignity. Understanding the impact that my diagnosis has can affect the client in multiple ways. Giving them their diagnosis can leave them feeling frustrated, confused, and unnerved, or it can be freeing due to the clarity that knowing brings. Knowing the impact of my words and how my clients move forward at times comes with a lot of pressure, but what allows me to do this work is knowing that the truth can set them free. Free from pain and trauma. Free from the strongholds that anxiety and depression have on them. Some people worry about the past while others are anxious about their future. Both can be paralyzing and leave you feeling stuck. Stuck and feeling that you aren't good enough and you don't have what it takes because you have failed before. Trauma has told us from the mouths and hands of our loved ones that where you are and what you have is it. It cannot get any better than this. No one is going to love you. You are not worthy of happiness. You are not strong enough to break the generational curses that have a strong hold on you and your family. But as a therapist, I am here to tell you that you can do anything you put your mind to. Anyone willing to put in the work with a motivated mindset can move a mountain. This mountain can be people, places, or things. It all starts with your mindset and how badly you are willing to fight for a life of meaning and purpose. You do not have to be a famous actor, athlete, or entertainer to accept and overcome life's challenges and live life beyond the diagnosis.

Facing Anxiety and Depression

My educational struggles due to anxiety and depression have deeply affected my experiences. Growing up in the 80s and 90s, schools were not focusing on mental health. Suffering from anxiety as a child and depression as a young adult heavily impacted my educational success. I now understand the trauma that led to these diagnoses and the determination it took to have a motivated mindset for education. My success was delayed but not denied. The key to turning lemons into lemonade and talking myself into the endless possibilities I could obtain required a positive mindset.

Reflecting on my childhood and watching all the older kids in the neighborhood go to school left me anxiously awaiting my turn. I could not wait until the day that I would be going too. The day finally arrived, and I remember walking to the bus stop holding my mom's hand with the biggest toothless smile on my face. What I did not realize was that I was not going to the same school as all my neighborhood friends; I was going to pre-kindergarten on the other side of town where few students and teachers looked like me and though I was excited, I was also scared. Upon the bus's arrival at the school, the bus driver with her long black hair and friendly smile turned to me and said, "Have a good day; I will be back to pick you up later." I flashed her my toothless smile, took a deep breath, and quietly said, "Okay."

Not sure where to go, I looked around and there was my mother. She had followed the bus to the school. I ran to her and jumped into her arms, and I knew everything would be all right. After a hug that I wish I could have held onto forever ended, she put me down, straightened up my dress and said, "Now let's go find your class." Walking into the school and seeing all the children, my excitement returned, and I was ready. We finally reached the door that had my name listed on it. As I walked into the class, I heard a loud, frustrated voice yell, "Take your seat and don't move until you are told to!" In that moment all the anxiety and fear returned. I looked back at the door and saw my mother's warm smiling face as she gestured to go in and find my seat. Upon finding my name tag and taking my seat, I looked back once more, and she gave me the thumbs up to say that everything was okay. Shell-shocked, I took my seat and did not move or speak. I just kept hearing the bus driver's voice in my head saying, "I will be back to pick you up later." That was my motivation to get through the day.

As a child, I associated being quiet with being good. Culturally, a child was to be seen and not heard. So, I decided that I would not talk at school so that my teacher wouldn't yell at me because I was being good. Also, I was paralyzed with fear from the sound of her yelling voice. As a child, I had no idea how this would impact my education.

My mother was unaware that I was not talking until the end of the school year when she came to pick me up early as she was signing me out at the office. The secretary, who was a customer of hers, stated, " I didn't know that your daughter was LD." My mother, not knowing what the initials meant, asked what that meant and she whispered, "Learning disabled." My mother, puzzled, immediately scheduled to meet with the teacher and principal to understand how her child was diagnosed without her knowledge or without making her aware of a concern. My mother could not understand what was happening because I was very talkative at home. I was experiencing anxiety due to the trauma and fear I was experiencing in the classroom. I was displaying "Selective Mutism" which is a mental health condition that causes people to be unable to speak in certain situations due to fear or anxiety.

As a mother, she knew that from this moment forward, she would have to show up for me by any means necessary. It was her mission to ensure that no one dimmed my light or quenched my spirit because I was created for a God-given purpose. Moving on to elementary school and back into my community, I was still afraid to talk. The traumatic experience of pre-kindergarten was not going to be easy to erase. I was still scared that I would be yelled at if I didn't have the right answer. Hearing my voice at times scared me because I didn't want to mess up. There was peace in knowing that my grandfather affectionately known as "Dada" was there. He was the custodian at the school. Whenever I felt nervous, I listened to him whistling in the hallway and it was our sign of comfort letting me know that I was not alone and that everything was okay. Not to mention that my aunt was a second-grade teacher at the end of the hallway.

Lessons from My Educational Struggles

By third grade, I finally had a teacher who made me feel special enough, good enough, and smart enough to be a scholar. Though I was shy then, she saw something in me that no other teacher had ever pulled out. She realized that working with me one on one allowed me to shine and just taking the time to build me up was all that it took for me to fly. I became a member of the safety patrol in elementary school and became a peer mediator in middle and high school. But this time my voice was once again misplaced. My high school guidance counselor made me feel like college was not an option for me and not a big deal. She allowed me to drop courses and slack off at the most crucial time in my education, which would allow me to go on to college. She encouraged and supported me in moving into study halls instead of calculus and chemistry courses which would have prepared me to compete with students across the nation. When it was time to apply for college, self-doubt came back and all the positive affirming and work that my third-grade teacher had put into me was once again erased. I struggled with completing the applications because in my head I could still hear my preschool teacher yelling, talking down to me, and discouraging me from being great.

Recognizing what was happening, my mother stepped up once again. She showed up for me, spoke on my behalf, met with the guidance counselor, and let her know that what she had done or did not do wasn't going to hold me back from my success. Not knowing much about college and its process, my mom believed that I had what it took to go. She trusted the judgment of my high school gym teacher who knew that I would benefit from attending a HBCU which stands for Historically Black Colleges and Universities. She felt it would be just what I needed to find myself, love myself, and most of all, find my voice again.

My parents had this bright idea to send me 8 1/2 hours away to college. Me, a girl who had never even spent the night down the street at her cousin's house. How funny was that?

After about a month of going to class, barely eating, and spending the rest of the time in my room, my neighbor in the dorm came and rescued me. I heard a knock at the door and my neighbor called my name and asked to come in. She sat on my bed and said, "Girl, something is wrong with you. You need to get out of this room and make the best of this time whether you want to be here or not." She forced me to get dressed and go hang out with her and her cousin. I know it should have been nice to get out, but all I wanted to do was go back to my room and hide under the covers. I felt like if I just went to sleep, the semester would go by faster.

Some time passed and my dorm neighbor came knocking once again, but this time she encouraged me to see a counselor to talk about my feelings and what I was going through. I have never done anything like this because I was always taught to talk to God and pray about it and everything would be all right. Where I'm from, therapy wasn't an option or even anything that black people considered. Talking about my feelings or even understanding that something was going on inside of me was all foreign to me, not to mention the counselor was a stranger. Prayer was my therapy and talking to a counselor was just weird. Being a first-generation college student, there was a lot of pressure on my success, and with a little brother behind me, I knew I couldn't fail. I didn't want to seem ungrateful for this opportunity because Lord knows I was too blessed to be depressed. My parents made major sacrifices to provide me with this opportunity, so I had to suck it up. How could I tell them that I was struggling? I did not want to seem like a quitter, or most of all, weak. At that time mental health in the African

American community was not something that was talked about.

Growing up in a Christian family you were always told to just trust God and know that you are never alone because He was always there. I was always taught the three P's: pause, pray, and proceed because you'll be alright. But this time was different. I was in a dark space and though I knew these things in my heart, my head could not fathom any of it. I could not get it together. I just could not shake it; each day became harder and harder to go to class and I started losing interest in things I once enjoyed. But I knew that I had to do the things that were required of me because my father left me with his famous words, "My money is a terrible thing to waste." This left me little room for error or failure. I knew that I had to figure it out.

Uncertain of what to expect or if this was going to help me, I took a chance because I just wanted to feel like myself again. I remember sitting there filling out the forms and not knowing how much or how little to say. How would she view me? How do I view myself putting these words on this paper? I trusted God had led me right where I needed to be so he would give me the words to say to express myself in the best way. The door opens and she calls me in. I can feel my heart beating out of my chest. I was full of anxiety and fear of being viewed as weak. I didn't know how to truly express what I was feeling inside or how to handle it. The counselor welcomed me with a smile and asked, "How are you today?" Immediately, I burst into tears. It was like the floodgates had opened and I didn't know if or when I would stop crying. Physically, my body had to release all of this built up trauma that I had no idea of how to deal with. She began to hug and console me in the way that my mother did back in pre-K on the first day of school. At that moment, I knew that everything would be all right. Needless to say, the first session didn't go very far, but a sense of peace and comfort was what I needed to know that I could continue. The following week, I went back feeling a little embarrassed, but at the same time feeling safe to say exactly what was on my mind and in my heart. Not once did she ever make me feel like I had lost my dignity. Following the intake, it was finally the moment of truth. I was diagnosed with depression. I finally had an answer to why I had been feeling the way that I was.

A million questions were running through my mind. A few that I remember were: What does this diagnosis mean? How do I explain this to my parents? How do I process this for myself? And what do I do now?

All I wanted to do was go back to hiding in my room, but I understood the importance of continuing to see my counselor. She encouraged me to share my diagnosis with professors and my family. She supported me in what was the hardest truth I ever had to share. Though she created a safe, nonjudgmental space for me to bear my truth, what would my professors say or how would this make my parents feel? She helped me understand that this was my life and my truth and that if God brought me to it, he would bring me through it, regardless of what everyone had to say or think. She poured into me until she was blue in the face helping me to see the importance of support.

The Power of a Village

I didn't know how to ask for support. I am supposed to have it together. I made it; I'm in college. I am a strong, independent black woman; I got this, or so I thought. It was not until my parents came to pick me up for Thanksgiving break that I realized I was not as good as I thought. This was the first time that they had seen me since they dropped me off in August when the semester began. Walking out of my dorm to my parents' car, the look on their faces when they saw me was so heartbreaking. I could hear my father saying, "Wow, look at her neck! She's all skin and bones!" For most college students, during the first semester they will gain about fifteen pounds. This is known as "the freshman fifteen." College students are known for having poor eating habits. Surviving off pizza, ramen noodles, and all types of junk food is where the weight picks up. They were expecting to see me slightly heavier but I had lost about 40 pounds within three months. I didn't look well according to the people who knew me best and now I had to share the reality of what was going on in my life.

Swallowing my pride and trusting my counselor's words, I had to tell them I was suffering from depression. But like most parents, they knew something was wrong just by looking at me. Being depressed I felt guilty and alone, but I was never alone. This was eye-opening for my parents and I. From that moment they made it clear to me that they would love me through anything and so would God. I gained support from my parents, family, and professors to persevere through the pressure of the depression. My ways of coping with this diagnosis started by acknowledging that I did not know exactly how to cope. I started keeping a calendar close by to track the number of days until I would be going home for break. My mother would call me daily to give me encouraging words. My dad called with daily dad jokes. His way of coping was laughing through the pain and there were times he had me laughing so hard I cried. In those times he would say, "These are the only tears I want you to cry." My parents even made monthly sacrifices to come visit and my mom would do my hair because she always said, "If you look better, you will feel better." They would send my little brother and cousin down to visit on their school breaks and it always just made me feel better to have a little piece of home on campus with me.

My counselor encouraged me to find things in the area that would give me the comfort of home. For starters, a good old-fashioned Baptist church would help. Though we had a chapel on campus, it was not the church vibe that I was used to. Finding a church where the preacher would "hoop" and the choir would "sang" along with the occasional praise break with tambourines being played and shouts of "Hallelujah!" and "Amen!" was what I needed. If you've been to a Baptist church, you know exactly what I mean.

Also, finding a radio station that played Latin music like Bachata, Merengue, and Salsa allowed me to close my eyes and escape back to my neighborhood which was full of life and culture. I never knew how much I would miss the sounds of the hustle and bustle of the inner city while living on a waterfront campus where it was quiet at night and all you could hear was the sound of crickets and the crashing waves of the water. When I think about it now, it makes me laugh. The peace that I was given was the thing that I wanted to get away from the most. I have never experienced quiet at that level and understanding that quiet was the thing that made my mind go places that I didn't necessarily want to go. Never having experienced that type of quiet, I did not know how much I had on my mind because the sound of the city always drowned it out.

The Power of Mindset

The most valuable insight that my counselor shared was the importance of alignment of my mind, body, and spirit. The balance of these three is the key to understanding myself in ways that I have never before. Positively affirming myself was also especially important in improving my mindset. She had given me the assignment of writing positive affirmations in each of my textbooks. Some of my affirmations included, "I am smart," "I am worthy of this experience," "I will graduate," and each semester I added more. If there was any doubt, confusion, or dark days, I would open a book and it would help me ground myself and be prepared for the studies ahead. I also wrote scriptures in each book. The scriptures that I chose were Revelations 3:8 (King James Version), "I know thy works: behold, I have set before thee an open door, and no man can shut it: for thou hast a little strength, and hast kept my word, and hast not denied my name," and Philippians 4:13 (King James Version), "I can do all things through Christ which strengthen me."

With prayer, persistence, and consistent counseling my light started to shine again. There is a saying on social media that the moment she believed in herself, the game changed. There is so much truth to this statement about my life and my educational journey. I became a first-year mentor to new students from Connecticut assisting them in getting acclimated to campus life and assisting them with locating resources. At times it may have been a home-cooked meal, a ride to Walmart, or just a conversation about things we missed from Connecticut. Understanding that my test was someone else's testimony made it all worth it.

Graduation Day: The Moment Everything Changed

Sunday, May 12, 2002, I made it to graduation. Hearing my name announced came with so many emotions. When I walked across that stage shaking the hands of some of the most important people on campus, the thing that meant the most was seeing my parents at the end of the stage. Best of all, my mother was there to greet me with a hug just like the first day of pre-K. At that moment, I knew that everything was all right because they were proud of me. They always knew that I could do it. It was one of the happiest days of my life, knowing that I completed one of the hardest tasks in my life because I had a motivated mindset.

A motivated mindset takes work and for many of us, we cannot achieve this without support. It takes a village to support the mental health of a child. Making sure that children are seen and heard is so important to their educational journey. It helps children understand their potential and the possibility of greatness is so important. It took my parents, grandparents, aunts, uncles, cousins, friends, bus drivers, teachers, professors, and counselors to keep me motivated. Everyone plays an important part, so don't miss the moment to encourage someone who may be in a dark place. It could be as simple as a smile to flip the switch back on and reignite the fire that each of us possesses and the key to unlocking a motivated mindset.

REFLECTIONS

What beliefs or mindsets have you had to challenge to grow and thrive?

Reflect on a time when courage led you to a breakthrough. How did it transform your life?

How can you actively cultivate a mindset of growth and resilience in your daily life?

Nardine Staroverov, LMFT

Beyond Borders: A Journey to Self

Nardine Staroverov, LMFT

Beyond Borders: A Journey to Self

"See, I am doing a new thing! Now it springs up; do you not perceive it? I am making a way in the wilderness and streams in the wasteland." - Isaiah 43:19 NIV

We often hear stories of immigrants that are painted in broad strokes and are reduced to tales of border crossing, deportations or poverty. Yet, at the heart of every immigrant's story lies a deeply personal journey-one fueled by hope and an unwavering desire for a better life. For many this journey represents a leap of faith that embodies both the promise of opportunity and the harsh realities of risks. The desire to build a better life for oneself and one's family is a powerful motivator.

Where I'm From: A Question of Identity

Where are you from? This question has and continues to bring up mixed emotions for me. Most people often lead with this question while in social settings to either make small talk or in an attempt to create connection with others. This question, at its core, is a question about identity. For some who have migrated to the United States as children, this question can often be associated with anxiety as they continue to struggle to integrate both cultures and gain a sense of solid identity formation, while attempting to navigate dual identities from country of origin and the new country.

Culture plays a crucial role in shaping children's health outcomes. For immigrant children, maintaining a strong connection to their cultural heritage can provide a sense of belonging and identity, which can help buffer the negative effects of acculturation stress. However, growing up, people associated Haitian immigrants with many negative stereotypes. We were often referred to as "boat people," or having some connection with the occult like Voodoo. Despite some of the stigma, my life experience was nothing like the media portrayed.

Immigration is a common practice especially for those living in developing and third world countries. It is not uncommon for family members, especially fathers, to leave their family behind and migrate to the United States in hopes of securing a job that would allow them to better care for their family members financially. It's also an opportunity to provide their children a better education. Immigration is an opportunity to provide financial and psychological stability as well as secure a better life for children.

What drives someone to leave their homeland - the place they have known their whole lives and leave everything they love behind? For some, it may be political instability, economic hardship, or persecution. Others might seek educational opportunities or reunification with family members. Regardless of the reasons, adjusting to a new country can be both exhilarating and overwhelming.

While there are many pros and cons to immigration, most don't stop to think about the experiences of young children and adolescents. While the parents may have one perspective, a child does not have the ability to decide whether they want to uproot their life and move to a different country. The move can feel abrupt, and the child may not have the ability to communicate feelings that relate to having to leave behind everything they have known.

What does immigration look like through the eyes of a child? Depending on a child's developmental stage, immigration can have various impacts on their emotional and psychosocial world. The experience of moving to a new country can be stressful and overwhelming for children, leading to increased levels of anxiety, depression, and other mental health issues. However, the process of acculturation can also have positive effects, such as increased resilience and adaptability. This is a story I know all too well.

Roots of Resilience

Growing up in Haiti is one of my fondest and happiest core memories. I grew up in a community that focused on collectivism. I can remember neighbors and family members stopping by and sharing meals together and laughing. Sundays were days where we attended church and visited family. Education was emphasized. But my most vivid memories were summers spent going to the countryside to visit my extended family and learning about agriculture while listening to my aunts and uncles share family stories. In the afternoon, my cousins and I would go down to the river and bask in the warm sun while sipping cool coconut water and munching on sweet quenepas, also known as Spanish limes. They are small, round fruits that grow on trees and are popular in many Caribbean countries. As the sun began to set, the rhythmic beats of drums filled the air, creating a captivating melody that echoed through the night inviting everyone to dance under the stars. But by the age of 10, all this would come to a complete halt.

I immigrated to the United States at the age of 10 years old along with my younger brother. Most of my father's family had already immigrated to the United States at least a decade before I arrived. Although reuniting with my family was exciting, I would soon learn about the impact of loss and shame as I learned to adjust and find my identity in a new country. My immigrant experience has impacted many facets of who I am today. But let's start from the beginning.

The Costs of Immigration

I was a happy child who loved school and thrived academically and socially. However, I would often dream about what it would be like to have my father around. I would often think of him especially when I was being disciplined by my mother. I would whisper to myself, "If only my father were here." Even though my mother is one of the gentlest human beings, I had this longing to know my father.

My father immigrated to the United States when I was three years old. I do not have any memories of him in Haiti aside from what I have been told by my mother. But one thing I did understand was that immigration was a huge part of my family history and it was normalized. At this point in my life, I had never met my paternal grandmother, or my aunts and my uncle from my father's side of the family because they had all migrated to the United States prior to my birth.

As a three-year-old at the time of my father's departure to the United States, my mother was pregnant with my younger brother. We were able to adjust as we lived in a tight knit community with friends and family. However, I missed out on building a bond with my father which is among the many losses I would face due to immigration. I would not see him again for another four years. When he did visit, the visit lasted for a week, but I have no recollection of any bonding moments with him.

Fast forward four years later, my mother was also granted a visa to relocate to the United States to join my father, however, my brother and I were not. At the time I was seven years old, and my brother was four. My mother had to make the difficult decision to leave her young children behind for the sake of gaining a better life. I wouldn't fully understand her experience and her sacrifice until I too became a mother.

The absence of one or both parents can have a significant impact on young children and adolescents' emotional and psychological wellness. Young children and adolescents can suffer from insecure attachments when one or both parents must leave them behind.

In my case, my mother left us in the care of her good friends. We would remain in Haiti for two and a half years before we were reunited with our parents. We were fortunate to have had a loving family to care for us. While our time with our host family was positive, we had lost complete connection with our parents for those two years, especially our mother who had been our safe person. Due to the poor infrastructure in Haiti, we did not have many options to communicate with our parents aside from sending recorded tapes with our voices.

Adjusting to a New World

At ten and six years old, my brother and I were waiting to board and finally take our long-awaited trip to reunite with our parents. Sitting at the airport in Haiti felt surreal. We were accompanied by our foster dad and our two foster siblings. My foster mom did not come to the airport as this goodbye was difficult for her. I remember walking to the wired fence that separated us and told my foster sister to tell my foster mom that I said goodbye. I did not realize and could not process the significance of this goodbye until many years later as I would never see her again.

I had dreamt about this day for years thinking about what it would look like to meet my paternal grandmother, my aunts, and cousins for the first time. I have this picture that my family sent us while we were in Haiti seared in my brain and pictured the same scene. I envisioned that my family would all welcome us in this spacious and beautiful living room while wearing their Sunday best. I soon realized that the scene I had pictured all those years was a photography studio.

When we arrived at JFK International Airport, it was overwhelming. I remember seeing so many different types of people. We were greeted by my parents and were quickly whisked away in a cab. The event of that day feels like a blur because I did not know how to make sense of all my emotions. I don't remember the drive to the apartment, but I do remember getting into a small room and it felt like I was transported from one space to another in what felt like a hallway. That was my first time in an elevator.

We finally arrived in my family's two-bedroom apartment in Brooklyn, New York where my grandmother, my aunt, her husband and their young daughter along with my parents all resided. This type of arrangement was normal for immigrant families. However, this was a stark difference for my brother and I coming from a home where we had our own rooms and a nanny. This was not at all what I had envisioned of my parents' life in the US.

We arrived during early summer and school was already out. I remember spending my days with my brother and younger cousins roaming the hallways of our building and watching "The Little Rascals" while our parents were off working, and my grandmother was home listening to her radio for political updates. I did not see much of my father during the week as he was working in Connecticut.

At the end of the summer, I was unaware that we were about to go through yet another transition and it was then that my process of acculturation and my identity was challenged. My parents decided to move to CT since my father had a full-time job there. I was anxious to start school, as my experience with school in Haiti was a huge part of my identity and I thoroughly enjoyed learning.

Due to my grades and academic level, I was placed in 6th grade even though I had just turned 10. On the first day of school, I was introduced to another girl who had just moved from Haiti and was also starting school that same day. I felt a sigh of relief and we became fast friends. However, for the first time in my life, school - a place where I always found solace - became a place of fear and trepidation.

Navigating Dual Identities

Walking to my first class felt overwhelming as I was experiencing a mix of anxiety, isolation and being surrounded by unfamiliar faces and sounds. It was also intimidating to see classmates who share the same language and cultural background. For the first time in my life, I felt "different." I was an outsider. I had never had to question whether I fit in based on the color of my skin, my economic status or my language. As the days went on,

I began to be more aware of my differences. I had experienced strange feelings that I had never experienced before.

I began to feel uncomfortable and insecure with my sense of self because I was made fun of for the way I dressed and my lips. School started becoming an unsafe space for me. Although I loved school, most of my energy was spent on becoming "invisible." I said to myself, "If I don't say anything, maybe they won't see me."

This strategy would not last very long as I became a target. I was not safe on the bus, in the locker room or even in the safety of a bathroom stall. This moment further solidified what the next few years would represent. During recess, I entered a bathroom stall, and I recall one of the girls who took pleasure in tormenting me leaning over my head. While I was in one of the most vulnerable states, the unthinkable happened. One of my usual tormentors scaled the bathroom stall, her eyes gleaming with mischief as her spit rained down in a cruel shower of humiliation. Before I could gather myself, I felt the warm liquid land squarely on my backside. As I lifted my head, I could see her face smirking back at me. I felt an extra layer of dread wash over me.

I felt such shame. I went home in tears and was absolutely devastated. I cried in secret and I did not share these encounters with my parents or teachers. Somehow, I thought I did something to incur these insults. "What was I doing wrong"? "Maybe I was not good enough", "I was not pretty enough". These were some of the thoughts that would continually invade my mind as I tried to make sense of my new world and my interactions with my peers.

I did not want my parents to be disappointed in me. This is one of the burdens of being an immigrant child. We often feel the need to make our parents proud because we understand the sacrifices that were made to allow us to have a better education and a chance at a successful life. But there's more to it. I was living with both of my parents for the first time that I could remember. I was transitioning at home and at school. I did not have the emotional safety to share such a vulnerable experience with my parents. I felt lonely at both home and school, so I pushed forward and dealt with the bullying and anxiety that came along with it.

Reestablishing a relationship with my father was a stressor. I feared him because I did not know how to navigate our relationship. My father then responded with despondence as he did not understand my fear. I simply did not know him. This lack of understanding did not allow us to build a relationship which further caused a loss for me. I had hoped for a relationship with my father and thought that I would simply be connected to him. Much to my surprise, my response was quite the opposite. I began to withdraw from my father, however, my bond with my mother did not dissipate.

As a 10-year-old who was mourning "home" this was a blow. I longed for acceptance and belonging, but it did not come. It was a painful feeling as if I did not have a space.

Academically, my parents were never the wiser. Even though I did not speak any English at the start of the school year, by the end of 6th grade I had a command of the English language. By 7th grade, my report cards were all A's and B's.

Although my grades did not suffer, I was no longer able to enjoy learning. My sense of self suffered because I was constantly in survival mode in school. When your brain is operating in survival mode, it does not allow space for creativity and can hinder learning. There are many parts of me that are lost because I was unable to explore those parts due to fear and anxiety. I still wonder who I would have been had I been given the opportunity to thrive. It reminds me of this C.S. Lewis quote, "You can't go back and change the beginning, but you can start where you are and change the ending."

At home, as I began to assimilate more as a preteen, I wanted things that began to challenge my family's values and norms. Although I desired certain experiences, I knew that it would not be accepted, so I just kept those longings to myself. While in 7th grade, my whole class attended Nature's Classroom, and I had to stay behind because my family did not believe in sending us off with people they didn't know. So, losing out on some of those experiences further alienated and kept me in the "other" category.

My parents had different sets of rules and expectations than our neighbors and peers at school who were not immigrants. I strived to be proud of my own culture by keeping up with my parents' expectations, but it was also difficult as I began to acculturate. While my parents were sending me a message that said, "don't become like them," I was also getting the message from my new culture that I didn't belong.

As middle school came to an end, I remember sitting on the floor of the room that I shared with my brother staring at the high school bus schedule and I muttered, "God, how can I survive four years?" I had to learn to detach emotionally and push through because I had no choice. I went through the motion of attending school and completing homework and projects, but I had no one to process my experiences and the feelings that were swallowing me up inside.

My new identity became "the shy girl," but I called it "selective mutism." I decided not to speak unless it was related to a homework assignment. This was my way of protecting myself. I remember a 10th grade assignment where we had to pick a poem and recite it in class. As I was reading an excerpt, I heard a voice saying, "She has a nice voice." I realized that some of my peers had never even heard my voice.

I was unaware of what anxiety felt like or how to identify it. Looking back, it's that little girl walking to the bus stop and crying because she did not know what her day was going to entail and trying to muster the courage to tackle another day. Anxiety was every time I passed a group of peers and prayed that I wouldn't make eye contact so that they wouldn't pick on me. I also struggled with suicidal ideation. However, I thought to myself, "I will not go to heaven if I do that." My spiritual beliefs were my saving grace.

Although I still find myself battling some triggers of anxiety today, I must continue to remind myself that I am resilient.

What does resilience look like? I did not allow anxiety to swallow me up. I pushed through and attended school every day and did my homework. I completed high school and obtained my bachelor's and master's degrees.

Despite the opposition, I always had a place of safety on the weekend, and this was my church family. The church provided me the opportunity to maintain a connection to my cultural heritage as it was a Haitian church. It was the space where I felt seen, valued and accepted. No one knew that Monday through

Friday was a nightmare. I longed for the weekend to come because it gave me a sense of relief. This space allowed me to have a voice - literally. I love to sing, and the church gave me a platform to display and develop my singing ability.

However, I still mourn the 10-year-old who missed out on dances and being part of a singing assembly because she was too fearful to try out. Instead she sang in the main choir where she could blend in. I mourn the girl who clipped her wings because she was afraid to fly.

As an adult, I continued to struggle and straddle the expectations of two cultures. When I went off to college, my goal was to make my parents proud and make sure they knew that their sacrifices were not in vain. When it came to a career, I was expected to engage in a career that involved health care. When I entered the social work field, I struggled because my parents did not understand the value of mental health and they did not think it would give me the financial stability I needed. I struggled and thought about going to medical school after earning my undergrad degree because I wanted to make my parents proud.

From Survival to Success

I decided to pursue my masters in Marriage and Family Therapy because my life experiences prepared me to serve those who are unseen. I also made peace with the idea of pleasing my parents because I understood that their experience was different from mine. They were coming from a scarcity mindset and were pursuing stability and financial security. They did not want me to experience the same struggles they endured. Because of their hard work, I was able to have a different experience and pursue a career that I was passionate about.

As mental health professionals, educators and policy makers, it is important to consider the cultural backgrounds of immigrant children when providing services and support. It is also important to assess the social-emotional needs of immigrant children. We are often so focused on language acquisition that we forget the whole child. A child who has immigrated is dealing with adjusting to a different school system, language, and cultural barriers.

In addition to these stressors, it's important to understand the child's support system. Some families may not fully understand how to meet the child's needs or how to advocate for their child in the school setting. It is up to educators and mental health professionals to recognize the importance of the whole child perspective and its impact on a child's identity formation and overall well-being.

Who am I today? I believe that my experiences are my greatest strengths. If I were to describe myself, I would say that I am Haitian born and have a strong connection to my cultural identity of being part of a collective community. I am also American based on how I live and operate. I am a little bit of both and somewhere in-between. I am a 1.5er-a term used to to describe people who immigrate to a new country during childhood or adolescence. Unlike first-generation immigrants who are born and raised in their home country and second-generation immigrants, who are born in the new country to immigrant parents, 1.5ers have a distinctive perspective.

I am still learning to embrace my dual identity. Being a 1.5er has become a strength rather than a weakness, as I practice self-compassion and give myself the space to explore what it means to be uniquely me. As educators, policymakers, and mental health professionals, we must create spaces where children navigating dual identities feel seen, heard, and supported. Only then can they move beyond survival and truly thrive.

REFLECTIONS

How has your cultural identity influenced your personal and professional life?

Reflect on a time when you broke through a significant barrier. What motivated you to persist?

How do you create spaces of belonging and acceptance for yourself and others in your community?

REFLECTIVE PROMPTS

Use these prompts to stimulate a deeper reflection, foster personal growth, and inspire you to take actionable steps in your mental health journey

Personal Resilience:
After reading Therapists Unmasked, what themes of resilience resonated most with you? How have your own experiences shaped your understanding of overcoming challenges?

Breaking Stigma:

How has this book changed your perspective on the stigma surrounding mental health? What steps can you take to contribute to normalizing conversations about mental health in your community?

Relatability and Connection:
Which story or moment in the book felt most relatable to you? Why do you think it stood out, and how can you apply its lessons to your own life?

Vulnerability as Strength:

Reflect on the idea that vulnerability is the foundation of strength. How can embracing your own vulnerability help you grow, heal, or connect with others?

Healing Strategies:

The authors shared strategies that supported their healing journeys. Are there any you feel inspired to try? How can you integrate these into your own path toward well-being?

Identity and Growth:
How has your identity played a role in shaping your mental health journey? What barriers have you faced, and how have they influenced your growth?

Creating a Legacy:

The authors are building legacies of resilience and advocacy. What legacy do you want to leave behind, and what steps can you take today to begin shaping it?

Supporting Others:

Reflecting on the stories you've read, how can you better support those around you who may be struggling? What actions can you take to foster connection and understanding?

Looking Ahead:

How do you plan to continue your journey of self-discovery and healing? What intentions can you set moving forward to maintain your mental well-being?

Gratitude and Growth:

Write a letter of gratitude to yourself, acknowledging how far you've come and the strength you've shown. Include aspirations for the person you are becoming.

MEET THE AUTHORS

Tangie R. McDougald, LPC

Visionary. Trailblazer. Advocate for Mental Health Transformation. Tangie R. McDougald is a Licensed Professional Counselor and an influential leader in the mental health field. As the founder and CEO of two distinguished mental health facilities in East Hartford, CT, Tangie specializes in trauma-focused therapy and elevating behavioral health standards. She holds a Master's in Mental Health Counseling from the University of St. Joseph and has built a legacy of empowering others through her expertise, philanthropy, and innovation.

A dynamic entrepreneur and creator, Tangie has pioneered several transformative projects aimed at normalizing mental health conversations and uplifting the industry. Her initiatives include:

The Ultimate Therapist Summit and Gala: A premier event celebrating excellence and empowering therapists to amplify their impact.

The Ultimate Therapists Mastermind: A sisterhood of clinical executives focused on scaling practices, fostering innovation, and building sustainable legacies.

The Reframe Magazine: A groundbreaking publication that reshapes narratives around mental health and wellness through inspiring stories and expert insights.

Therapists Unmasked: True Stories of Resilience, Transformation, and Breaking Barriers Beyond a Diagnosis: Her latest anthology project, highlighting the human side of mental health professionals while breaking stigmas and fostering hope.

As a three-time Amazon Best-Selling Author, Tangie is committed to using her voice and platform to challenge mental health disparities, advocate for change, and create spaces for healing and connection. Her efforts have earned her recognition as a Business and Community Leader in the Hartford Courant's Best of Hartford Readers Poll for three consecutive years (2021–2023).

In addition to her clinical and entrepreneurial accomplishments, Tangie serves as Co-Chair of the Route 2 Collaborative, supporting community mental health practitioners with essential resources. She is also a proud wife, mother, and "Glam-Ma" to two wonderful grandsons. Guided by her personal mantra, "IT'S PERSONAL," Tangie embodies the spirit of social change, leaving a lasting legacy of resilience, transformation, and progress.

Connect with Tangie:

Website: www.communitymattersopcc.com

Instagram: iamdr.tangie

LinkedIn: Tangie R. McDougald, NCC, LPC

Join her private Facebook group: The Ultimate Therapist

Schedule a consult: www.calendly.com/iamtangie

Yvonne Sailor-Walker, LPC

Yvonne Sailor-Walker was born and raised in Hartford, CT. She was raised by a host of family members including her maternal grandmother, paternal grandmother and aunts. Each of these individuals played a pivotal role in her life shaping her into the woman that she is today.

Yvonne is a licensed professional counselor and CEO of Radiant Life Psychotherapy, LLC located in both Georgia and Connecticut. She's an Amazon bestselling author as well as a public speaker, and she enjoys speaking about her passions - church, prayer, and therapy. She is certified in DBT, Substance Abuse, Sex Offender Trainer Certified, and Anger Management, as well as works with couples, adults, children, and teens in her private practice. Yvonne has a passion for giving back to the community and recently expanded Radiant Life to Georgia where she offers community support services to those in need. Yvonne has overcome so many barriers throughout her life which include sexual assault, physical, verbal, and emotional abuse, as well as going through the Foster Care system. Trauma has left her feeling isolated, devalued, broken, anxiety-ridden, hopeless, heartbroken, suicidal, and unlovable. This was all before God showed up and showed her who she was and to whom she belonged.

Yvonne is a mother to five wonderful children - two biological, two stepchildren, one adopted baby boy, and played a part in helping raise her two cousins as a Relative foster parent. She is also a wife of 19 years to a phenomenal, supportive husband and father to her children. She wants her readers to know that there is still hope in Jesus and prayer changes things. She shares her journey through healing so transparently and courageously that she hopes her readers will be left feeling hopeful and encouraged. Yvonne shares how both therapy and prayer changed her entire life, and as a result, she is no longer defined by her past, or what others negatively spoke over her life. Because she has been transformed through prayer and therapy, she can now walk in her purpose and calling. She can be the therapist and woman of God that she was called to be. The joy of walking in your true calling is an indescribable feeling that she hopes and prays each one of her readers will seek and experience.

Connect with Yvonne at:

Website: www.radiantlifepsychotherapy.org

Email: ysailor@radiantlifepsychotherapy.org

Facebook: YvonneSailor

Instagram: radiantlife_wog

Tawanna Marie Woolfolk, MSW, LCSW

With over 21 years of clinical experience specializing in complex trauma treatment and integrated wellness services, Tawanna Woolfolk is a licensed clinical social worker with a MSW from Smith College School of Social Work. Woolfolk is certified as an EMDR therapist, Trauma Professional, and Grief Specialist. She is in private practice at Sacred Ground Institute, LLC where she is also the director and CEO. Tawanna grew up in the foster care system after suffering malnutrition, educational neglect, sexual and physical trauma. Tawanna always intuitively knew who the right people were to steward her through towards resiliency and has committed her life to planting mustard seeds of hope and faith through her clinical work, public speaking, training, education, advanced clinical supervision and consultation.

Connect with Tawanna at:

Personal Email: tmw6328@gmail.com

Business Website: www.sacredgroundinstitute.com

Public Facebook Profile: tawannamariewoolfolk

Business Instagram: sacredgroundinstitute

Business LinkedIn: tawannamariewoolfolk,LCSW

Dr. Tasha N. Rose, LPC

Dr. Tasha N. Rose, DHSc, LPC, is the owner and CEO of Let's Talk About It Counseling Services. She specializes in transformative counseling, employing a holistic approach that integrates scripture, prayer, humor, and clinical techniques. Her comprehensive method aims to induce an out-of-body experience and foster a positive outlook on self and life.

Tasha addresses shame, guilt, and unforgiveness, guiding clients toward affirmation, assurance, liberation, safety, and inspiration for positive change through love and forgiveness. Her ideal clients are those seeking spiritual growth with a willingness to explore and understand God's will. Emphasizing accountability and completing assignments, she facilitates a transformative process she terms the "Unconscious Healing" experience, utilizing pillars like faith, forgiveness, accountability, intention, transparency, and general healing.

Tasha's journey into counseling is a deeply personal one, rooted in a lifelong empathy for others' pain. This recognition of her ability to offer support and guidance led her to pursue mental health counseling in 2010. Her understanding of the intersection of spiritual and mental warfare further deepened her commitment, leading her to establish Let's Talk About It Counseling Services, LLC in 2019. Her calling to serve individuals seeking spiritual counseling is the driving force behind her work.

With a Doctorate of Health Science, certified in Advanced Trauma-Informed Counseling, Tasha is a highly qualified and experienced counselor. Her commitment to continuous learning and staying updated with the latest research and practices in the field is a testament to her dedication to her clients. Her strong foundation in both spiritual knowledge and formal education positions her to guide clients toward self-acceptance and life aligned with their values and beliefs.

You can connect with Dr. Rose at:

Email: Info@letstalkaboutitcounselingct.com

Website: www.Letstalkaboutitcounselingct.com

Fcaebook: TashaRose

Instagram: letstalkaboutitcounseling

Linkedin: Dr.TashaRose,LPC

Tawana L. Preston, LMSW

Tawana Preston was born and raised in Meriden, Connecticut. Her parents instilled in her the importance of having a motivated mindset early on. They taught her that she could do and be anything she put her mind to. Through life's challenges, she held onto their words and persevered.

She holds a Bachelor of Science degree in Marketing from Hampton University and worked as a Marketing Coordinator in the wireless technology industry for a decade. Times changed and so did her career. She decided to join the family business and became a licensed cosmetologist. As an award-winning hairstylist, she realized it did not matter how beautiful she was able to make her clients on the outside if they had unresolved internal trauma. Coming to this realization and her passion for people's well-being inspired her to return to graduate school in 2020 at the University of Saint Joseph in pursuit of her master's degree in social work.

It was at this moment Tawana understood that she had finally found her true calling. She was recognized as the 2022 National Association of Social Workers Connecticut Chapter Student of the Year and the Executive Board President for her 2023 Master of Social Work Cohort.

She has participated in major research on the topics of the role of social media and storying experiences of campus sexual assault and COVID-19 pandemic's impact on college students' well-being. Being a student during the height of the pandemic she was her own best subject in how a motivated mindset fosters resilience and perseverance.

Tawana's current career as a licensed master social worker allows her to meet clients and students where they are and expose them to the endless possibilities they have to offer the world with help and healing. She is passionate about working with adults looking to tap into their resilience through strength-based and client-centered therapeutic approaches. She is also a Care Specialist assisting community college students in creating college/life balance. In her role, she addresses the students' needs for resources in the area of basic needs, mental health, wellness, and scholarships. She is most proud of her work as a mother to a teenage daughter who is following in her footsteps as a National Honor Society student. In 2020, she also founded a virtual prayer group "Team Faith." Her unwavering faith in God has sustained her in both good and tough times but her motivated mindset is what keeps her going because this is just the beginning of all she will become!

Connect with Tawana at:

Facebook: tawanapreston

LinkedIn: tawana-preston-165799b5

Instagram: tawana324

Email: socialworkerofpurpose@gmail.com

Nardine Staroverov, LMFT

Nardine Staroverov is a licensed marriage and family therapist with 15 years of experience in the field of mental health. Nardine specializes in couples therapy where she helps them navigate the trauma of betrayal and restore their relationship to a healthier emotional dynamic.

Nardine was born in a small town in Limbe, Haiti. She immigrated to the United States at the age of 10. Her experiences living in Haiti have given her a love for storytelling. She has always been fascinated by other people's stories, especially that of her extended family.

The love of storytelling led her to participate in a research project for a book entitled "Becoming a Teen Mom: Life Before Pregnancy" written by Mary Patrice Erdsmans and Timothy Black at the Center for Research at the University of Hartford. This experience allowed her to understand the many struggles that teen moms faced beyond the socially constructive narrative of those who may be out of touch.

Her experiences as an immigrant child have also had a profound impact in her identity formation. This has led her to be more empathetic to people who may be considered an "underdog" and ultimately into the field of mental health.

Nardine completed her bachelor's degree in Human Development and Family Relations at the University of

Connecticut and subsequently received a master's degree in Marriage and Family Therapy at Central Connecticut State University.

When Nardine is not sitting on the couch with couples, she's spending time with her husband and her three beautiful children. She also enjoys traveling and indulging in a good glass of wine with her girlfriends.

Connect with Nardine at:

Email: Nardine@hopespeaksllc.com

Website: www.hopespeaksllc.com

Facebook: hopespeaksllc

Instagram: Hopespeaks_couneling

RESOURCES

READING LIST

Explore these books, which focus on mental health, resilience, identity, and healing—particularly for people of color. These works blend personal stories, professional insights, and culturally relevant approaches to mental well-being:

MENTAL HEALTH AND SELF-CARE:

The Unapologetic Guide to Black Mental Health
Dr. Rheeda Walker

A practical guide for navigating mental health, reducing stigma, and finding culturally sensitive care.

Sister Outsider
Audre Lorde

A collection of essays and speeches that explore identity, resilience, and the intersection of race, gender, and mental health.

Mindful of Race: Transforming Racism from the Inside Out
Ruth King

Explores mindfulness as a tool to confront racial bias and foster healing and compassion.

MENTAL HEALTH RESOURCES

Below is a list of professional organizations, hotlines, and websites to support readers on their mental health journeys:

CRISIS HOTLINES:

National Suicide Prevention Lifeline (U.S.): 1-800-273-TALK (8255) or 988

Crisis Text Line: Text HOME to 741741

International Suicide Hotlines: For a comprehensive list, visit Befrienders.org.

THERAPY RESOURCES:

Psychology Today's Therapist Directory
www.psychologytoday.com/us

Therapy for Black Girls (U.S.)
www.therapyforblackgirls.com

Inclusive Therapists
www.inclusivetherapists.com

ADDITIONAL RESOURCES

As you continue your journey toward resilience, healing, and transformation, these resources are designed to support your growth and deepen your understanding:

1. Beyond the Diagnosis Workbook: A Guided Journey to Resilience, Healing, and Transformation

This workbook is the perfect companion to Therapists Unmasked. It offers reflective prompts, guided exercises, and actionable strategies to help you navigate life's challenges and build a foundation for growth and well-being.

Learn more or purchase your copy at:
www.tangiemcdougald.com

2. The Reframe Magazine

A transformative publication focused on reshaping the narrative around mental health and wellness. Each issue includes inspiring stories, expert insights, and practical tools to empower you on your mental health journey.

Subscribe or find the latest issue at:
www.thereframemag.com

"Your healing journey is uniquely yours. These resources are here to support you as you navigate, grow, and thrive—beyond the diagnosis."

REFERENCES

Hartmann, H. (2020). *Annihilation Anxiety: Understanding and Treating the Fear of Nonexistence.* Psychoanalytic Inquiry, 40(2), 147-160.

Kalsched, D. (2013). *Trauma and the Soul: A Psycho-Spiritual Approach to Human Development and Its Interruption. Routledge.*

Laing, R. D. (1960). *The Divided Self: An Existential Study in Sanity and Madness.* Penguin Books.

Winnicott, D. W. (1960). *The Maturational Processes and the Facilitating Environment: Studies in the Theory of Emotional Development.* International Universities Press.

Freud, S. (1926). *Inhibitions, Symptoms and Anxiety.* International Psycho-Analytical Press.

Hartmann, H. (2020). *Annihilation Anxiety: Understanding and Treating the Fear of Nonexistence.* Psychoanalytic Inquiry, 40(2), 147-160.

Kalsched, D. (2013). *Trauma and the Soul: A Psycho-Spiritual Approach to Human Development and Its Interruption.* Routledge.

Stern, D. (2010). *The Interpersonal World of the Infant: A View from Psychoanalysis and Developmental Psychology.* Basic Books.

www.ingramcontent.com/pod-product-compliance
Lightning Source LLC
LaVergne TN
LVHW022217200926
848481LV00006B/2009